VIATICUM

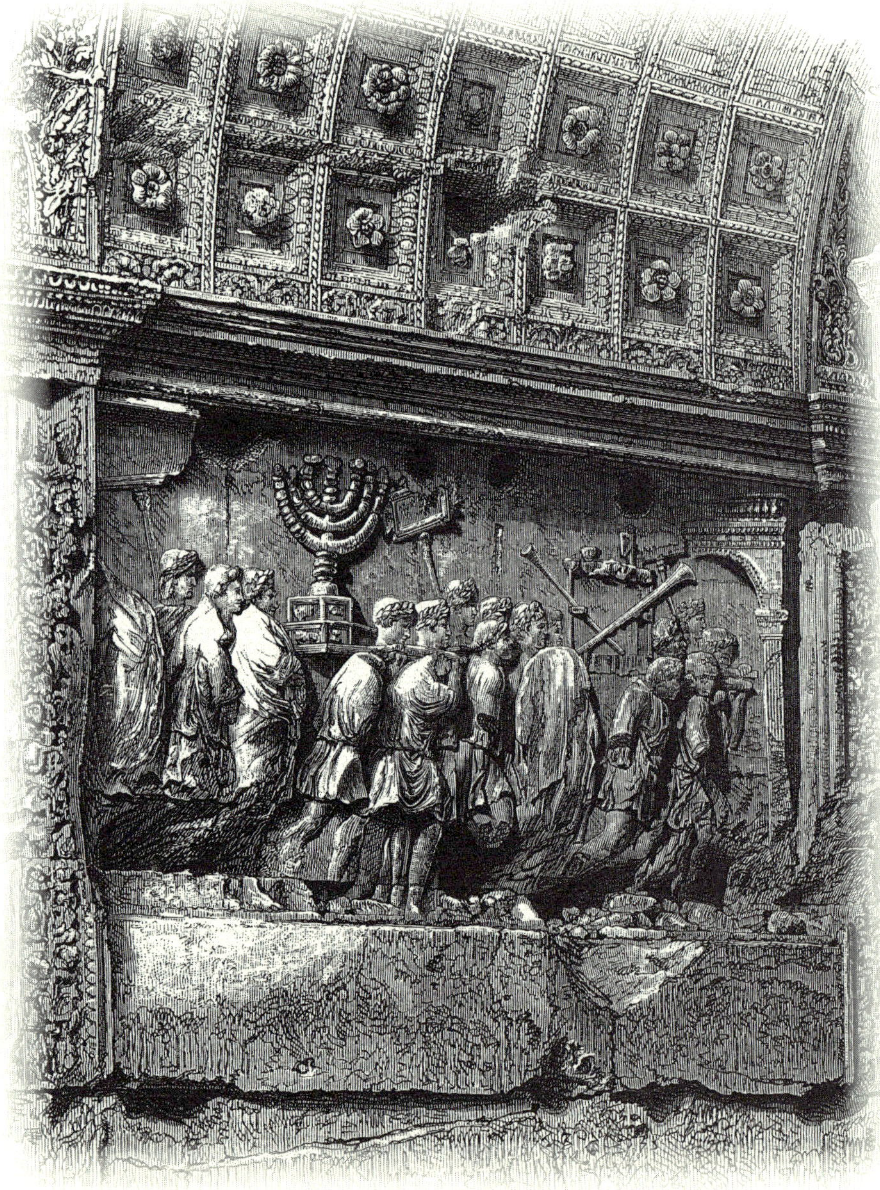

VIATICUM

FROM NOTEBOOKS

Jeffery Donaldson

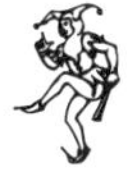

The Porcupine's Quill

Library and Archives Canada Cataloguing in Publication

Title: Viaticum : from notebooks / Jeffery Donaldson.

Names: Donaldson, Jeffery, 1960– author.

Identifiers: Canadiana 20190071370 | ISBN 9780889844223 (softcover)

Subjects: LCSH: Donaldson, Jeffery, 1960—Notebooks, sketchbooks, etc.

Classification: LCC PS8557.O527 V53 2019 | DDC C818/.54—dc23

1 2 3 • 21 20 19

Published by The Porcupine's Quill, 68 Main Street, PO Box 160, Erin, Ontario N0B 1T0. http://porcupinesquill.ca

Represented in Canada by Canadian Manda.
Trade orders are available from University of Toronto Press.

We acknowledge the support of the Ontario Arts Council and the Canada Council for the Arts for our publishing program. The financial support of the Government of Canada through the Canada Book Fund is also gratefully acknowledged.

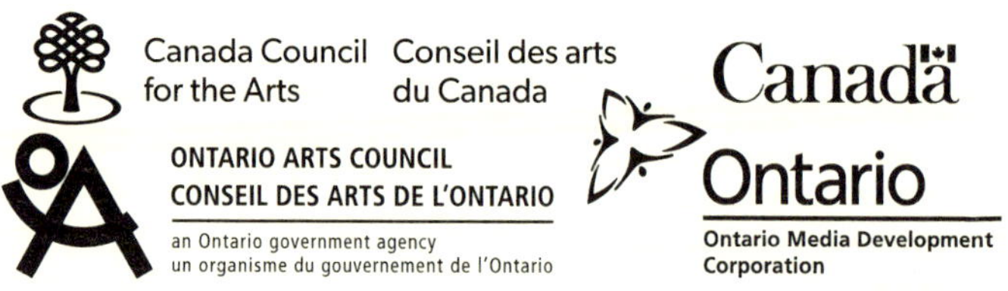

Celui qui a été ne peut plus
désormais ne pas avoir été:
désormais ce fait mystérieux
et profondément obscur d'avoir vécu
est son viatique pour l'éternité.

—Vladimir Jankélévitch

List of Illustrations

The cover image is a woodcut from *Daß Narrenschyff ad Narragoniam*, a satirical allegory published in 1494 in Basel, Switzerland, by the theologian Sebastian Brant. This particular image is attributed to the so-called Haintz-Nar-Meister. Digital colourization by Stephanie Small.

The frontispiece presents a detail from the Arch of Titus on the Via Sacra, Rome, just to the southeast of the Roman Forum.

I. A bridge below Gavarnie in the Hautes-Pyrénées, France.

II. The Erechtheion is a Greek temple on the north side of the Acropolis, dedicated to both Athena and Poseidon.

III. Interior of the Colosseum, Rome.

IV. Entrance to the Hall of the Ambassadors in the Alhambra Palace, Granada, Spain.

V. Saint-André church in the village of Luz-Saint-Sauveur was built in the 12th century, then later fortified by the Knights Hospitallers of the Order of St John of Jerusalem.

VI. Off the Rialto, Venice.

VII. The gardens of the Kremlin, Moscow.

VIII. Part of an aqueduct near Tivoli.

The engravings, with the one exception of the cover image, are reproduced from *Picturesque Europe*, Cassell & Company, London (circa 1875).

Preface

Writing escapes me. Let me get that out of the way. I never know how to write. I don't know how to begin writing and I don't know how to keep writing once I've begun. I don't understand momentum. I don't understand how words go together; I don't know how they come right, or how (and whether) I know it when they do. They are Scrabble games, our poems, our novels and essays. The little tray of letters and words and sounds and ideas and images: something gets spelled out, and it goes from there. It's always your move.

I could leave well enough alone, but words escape me in the other sense. Mine is the prison warden's peculiar laziness: I keep words locked up within, sit passively over them, keep them in their cells. What could they have done that was so awful? Occasionally I let them out in exercise yards that are no bigger than a notebook. They pace, they lie quietly in their narrow rooms. Most of the time they behave well enough. But come certain mornings, when I go in to check, I find empty spaces, a hole in a wall, a narrow tunnel leading out into the fields beyond. They won't be kept away from where they want to be. They want to be about. I think, don't worry I'll find them, I'll round them up and get them to march in line. But not before they have done some further mischief.

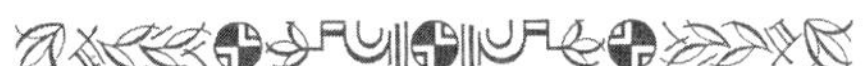

I am fascinated with openings, brilliant starters, brilliant non-starters. 'Mrs Dalloway said she would buy the flowers herself.' 'April is the cruellest month.' What? How do they know? A first musical phrase, a first brush on the canvas, a first word. There is not anything, then out of nowhere an inkling proposes itself.

A window onto a world. Or rather, a window onto a world and the world itself that you see through that window. Both at once. Wallace Stevens got it right:

> The way the earliest single light in the evening sky, in spring,
> Creates a fresh universe out of nothingness by adding itself.

With an audacity that only newborns and children understand, it allows itself to be what it is, just to see what happens. There is a strange ambivalence in that first appearance: a *certain* unfolding in an *uncertain* direction.

All sorts of people keep notebooks. I know friends who have them and while I long to take a peek I know that their disinclination to think of them as works in themselves is admirable and appropriately modest. I think of notebooks the way Elizabeth Bishop thought of account books. She said, 'Account books? They are dream books.' It is the daily work of trying to 'account' for things, first salvos, sketches that you keep to yourself. Beginnings in a sense are provisions for a journey, at the very least because every journey has a beginning that quite actually provides for it. What journey might a whole bunch of beginnings provide for? I began to wonder about my own writing habits, how my notebooks seemed, as Bishop says about her account books, 'honeycombed with zeros'. Never quite the actual first number. But there they were, giving the appearance of adding themselves up.

What are they to become? When does a thought become part of a poem and when does it become part of some other form of writing? Is it grounded in images whose alliances will be more metaphoric and intuitive? Or does it tend towards an intelligible logic that wants to say something? How in the end are these even different? 'The poet never lieth because he nothing affirmeth,' writes Sir Philip Sidney. Says W.B. Yeats: 'You can refute Hegel but you can't refute the song of sixpence.' When are my notes trying to become irrefutable poems and when are they sticking their necks out, so to speak, and making a claim? The stakes seem crucial to me, even though the form of the writing itself seems, at least at first (at second? at third?) strangely the same. You jot something down and watch to see how it leans.

Some of these pages have clearly decided which way they want to go, though for me they still hold within them phrases that might have pointed them in another direction, towards another reason for being. Many of them I think hang in the balance, extended reflections drifting away from some poetic kernel, not yet having reached their point of no return. They are 'false starts', not because the start was untimely, but because they don't go past starting. How to embody that special state of mind that Stevens called 'a readiness for first bells'?

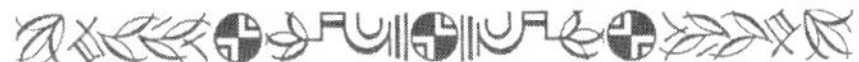

I love books of aphorisms. James Merrill writes in his poem 'The Broken Home': 'I have thrown out yesterday's milk / And opened a book of maxims.' He is getting at that sense, in collections of verbal zingers, of wanting to discard the dross in one's life and start again from first principles. It is a tradition that includes Pascal's everlasting *Pensées*, but more recently the Romanian writer E.M. Cioran's volumes of think pieces (*Drawn and Quartered*, *Anathemas and Admirations*). Here at home, we have George Murray's witty adages in his two recent books *Glimpses* and *Quick*, and Stephen Heighton's excellent rigours and workables in his *Workbook*. There may be something in the water these days, in the zeitgeist, that favours hints and guesses.

Murray thinks of his 'quicks' as being poems boiled down, a rarefication. I like that. I think of my ventures as more preliminary and undecided, sometimes too little and sometimes too big for their britches. But through them I like to think of how things come to be, how they end, and where they go when they do both.

I provide sections of loose thematic relation that fold back into one another as the pages unravel. Otherwise, I think of this book as beginning and ending nowhere, as a possible provision, in the spirit and in honour of the author whose quotation opens this volume.

I

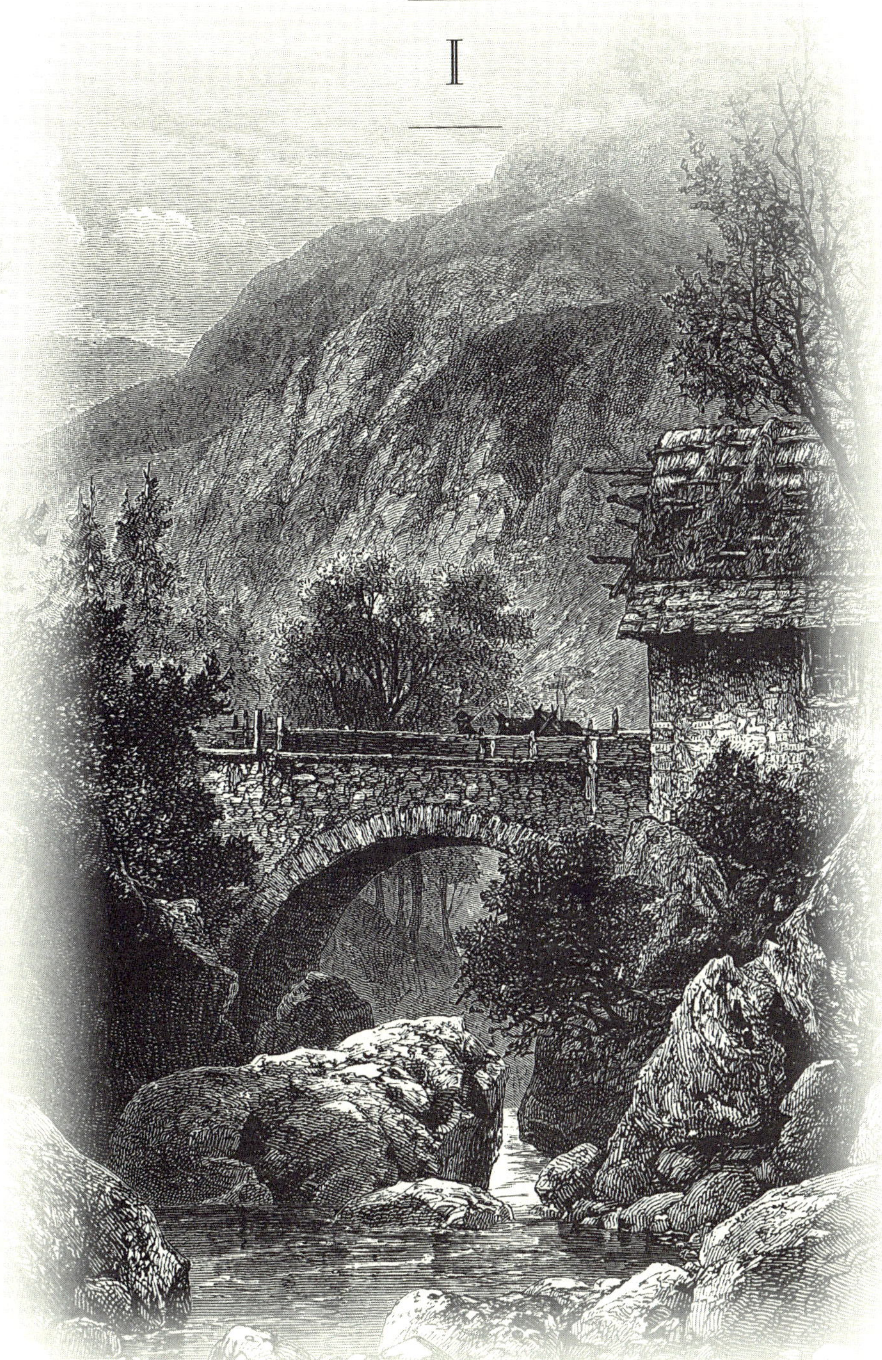

For a story. The day they brought Virginia Woolf back to life so that she could see what had become of her London. But very visceral. They exhume the body, lift what is left of the flaky-fleshed bones from the coffin in the middle of, say, Piccadilly Circus and breathe life into her. She is confused, doesn't recognize herself, looks down at her bone wrists, at the little bit of dried skin still stuck to her left knee, at the ruin of herself, and is distracted, can't really take in what she might otherwise see of our later world around her. She is a child woken in the middle of the night, disoriented, groggy. There are technicians in white lab coats holding her up in a sitting position because she cannot hold herself. The experiment is a failure.

I'm reading this little book on Proust where the author talks about the narrator's faith *à la magie des mots à leur pouvoir d'invocation.* The power of invocation in the magic of words. I keep coming back to Frye's saying that he was always just looking for 'the right verbal formula'. That last word sticks in my head. I'd always thought of 'formula' more as mathematical equation than as recipe, but there is something of both in it. Math tries to measure and mark down the reality of something abstract and invisible. The recipe tries to make, conjure, cook up. The right verbal formula: when you finally find it, something comes to be, something *happens.* The whole history of alchemy there.

On the actualizing power of words. Compare Isaiah 55:10–11:

For as the rain cometh down, and the snow from heaven, and returneth not thither, but watereth the earth, and maketh it bring forth and bud, that it may give seed to the sower, and bread to the eater: So shall my word be that goeth forth out of my mouth: it shall not return unto me void, but it shall accomplish that which I please, and it shall prosper in the thing whereto I sent it.

There is a mystery there. I say in the imperative, 'Hand me that book', and like magic you hand me the book. The word prospered in the thing whereto I sent it. But what of the power of imaginative language? Keats says, 'I stood tip toe upon a little hill', and in saying he makes it so. It is a subtler prospering in the thing whereto Keats sends it. It's all there in the Genesis creation story: God says, 'Let there be light', and there is light. He doesn't command light to start being. He speaks in the optative: '*Let* there be light.' He makes an allowance for light, which light may then come to occupy. The making of the allowance *is* the summoning. That funny moment when the magician onstage, as he speaks the conjuring formula 'abracadabra', performs a wide sweep of the arm. We speak the poem aloud but what we don't see is the wide sweep of the arm.

Our investment in the reality of illusion. We say of a fiction that it never really happened, and lay it aside. In physics, we say Newton's theories seemed to be accurate, based on appearances at the time, but that now we must understand them in the context of quantum variables and vibrating strings. They are not so much laid aside—they still have their practical uses—as contained inside a larger perspective. We have a harder time granting that allowance in literature. Newton still gets to be a rock star, while the song of sixpence gets patted on the head.

But quantum physicists are nearer the point of convergence in the two disciplines. They recognize that a theory, say, of quantum entanglement reveals not what is out there primarily, but the conditions of mind that reveal the world as such. Even when that mind hits a wall it isn't like there is something 'more true' on the other side. Heisenberg says that the world reflects back to us our means of questioning it. Poets, come out from your hiding places.

Effective disinterested contemplation is possible only with illusions that have been recognized as illusions, illusions that forgo the power to entice us into belief and so delay the question of action. This is another way of saying that contemplation's relation to what it makes happen is entirely metaphorical.

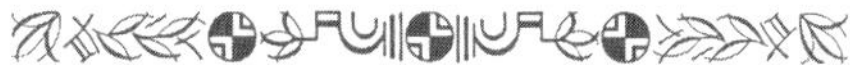

The models of science are really intended to do the same kind of work as ancient myths, i.e., prove prophetic in their ability to predict the future and to consolidate a culture around its particular way of measuring and describing our basic needs. Aeneas going into the underworld to hear from his father, Anchises, about the Roman history that was to follow. The model of the atom is both a measure of what has been and a prediction of cause-and-effect events to come. Hence, prophetic. The prophecy of myth is the order of what has happened dressed up as the order of what will happen again. Same in physics.

This mind candy, the theory of simulated universes as based on pure probabilistic reasoning. If there are potentially an unlimited number of universes, there would have to be universes that were capable of simulating universes artificially or by 'computer'. And since it would be easier to simulate a universe than to make a real one, there would theoretically have to be more simulated universes than actual universes. Hence, based strictly on odds, it is likelier that we inhabit one of those simulated universes. Down the rabbit hole.

But it's fun to think about the question of origins in such a universe. One possibility in a simulated universe is that you could start it anywhere and any time you like. You could create a world *in medias res*, a world for instance that begins only this moment, and you could design it such that the past that we believe preceded us, even our own personal past, even the past of earlier today, is an illusion programmed into the simulation. We would only be 'just here', 'just now'. My setting out to write this note at the top of this paragraph didn't really happen. I've been designed to think that I remember it happening.

We know a place is the actual world when the only way out of it is imaginary. Death, I'm talking about you.

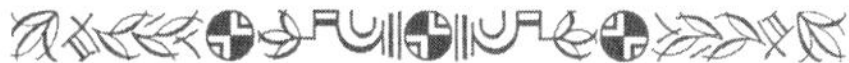

Buildings are like novels and stories, or letters and ephemera from the past, addressed to us. The city becomes a library archive. We move among the narrow shelves high above our heads. A man enters a building, a reader opens a book.

Saying that religions or other myths are untrue is like saying that a bridge over a river is untrue, or that cutting through a mountain to build a road is untrue. No engineer would make a road that suited the contours of the land at every turn. We do not accuse them of lying, falsifying the facts of the land. Indeed much of our practical science is exactly this building of more expedited and convenient means of getting somewhere, an insistence on 'we would have it so'. A bridge is a form of story. Those crossing the bridge are readers of the story. They go with it.

Thinking of the genius of the lucid dreamer, who, the moment he realizes he is dreaming, simply takes flight, or conjures heaven. In normal dreams, you don't say to yourself, 'I'm dreaming'. You simply generate the path that you walk along and imagine it is an actual path, separate from yourself. You fall obligingly into the hole that you yourself put there. It shows how asleep we are when we are awake.

I keep coming back to it, that reason is a form of story, but where we feel that the leaps of cause-and-effect logic are something more than metaphorical. We call those leaps reasonable, but the circularity merely disguises the mystery of the leap itself.

We live inside our imagined fictions, our stories. We move in them the way dancers move inside a dance. The dance itself is pure form, but actual bodies go *through* their motions and make them look like things that can be danced.

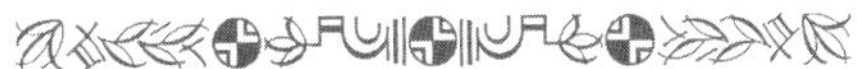

Book IX of the *Republic*. In response to the point that the ideal state exists nowhere on earth, Socrates replies: 'It makes no difference whether it exists or will ever come into being … there is a pattern of it laid up in heaven for him who wishes to contemplate it and so beholding to constitute himself its citizen.' I wonder about that phrase 'and so beholding to constitute himself' and what it suggests about how the realities we create in poems might in some manner be actualized. The beholding is a making it so, and a living there.

Theatres are a kind of desert: places of mirage and illusion. The condition of being that gives rise to them: desert land.

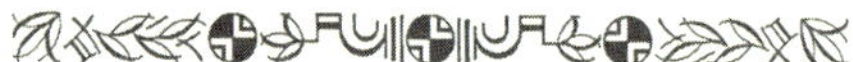

As walking is a description of the laws of gravity, so speaking is a description of the laws of language.

This question again of whether societies can actually change themselves, make new spaces to move into. I keep coming back to *Harold and the Purple Crayon*, about the toddler with the big crayon in his hand who quite actually draws the world around him: draws the bed he will lie down in, draws the railroad tracks he will set out upon, and of course draws himself in the process of entering the thing he is drawing. Poems as a kind of purple crayon.

II

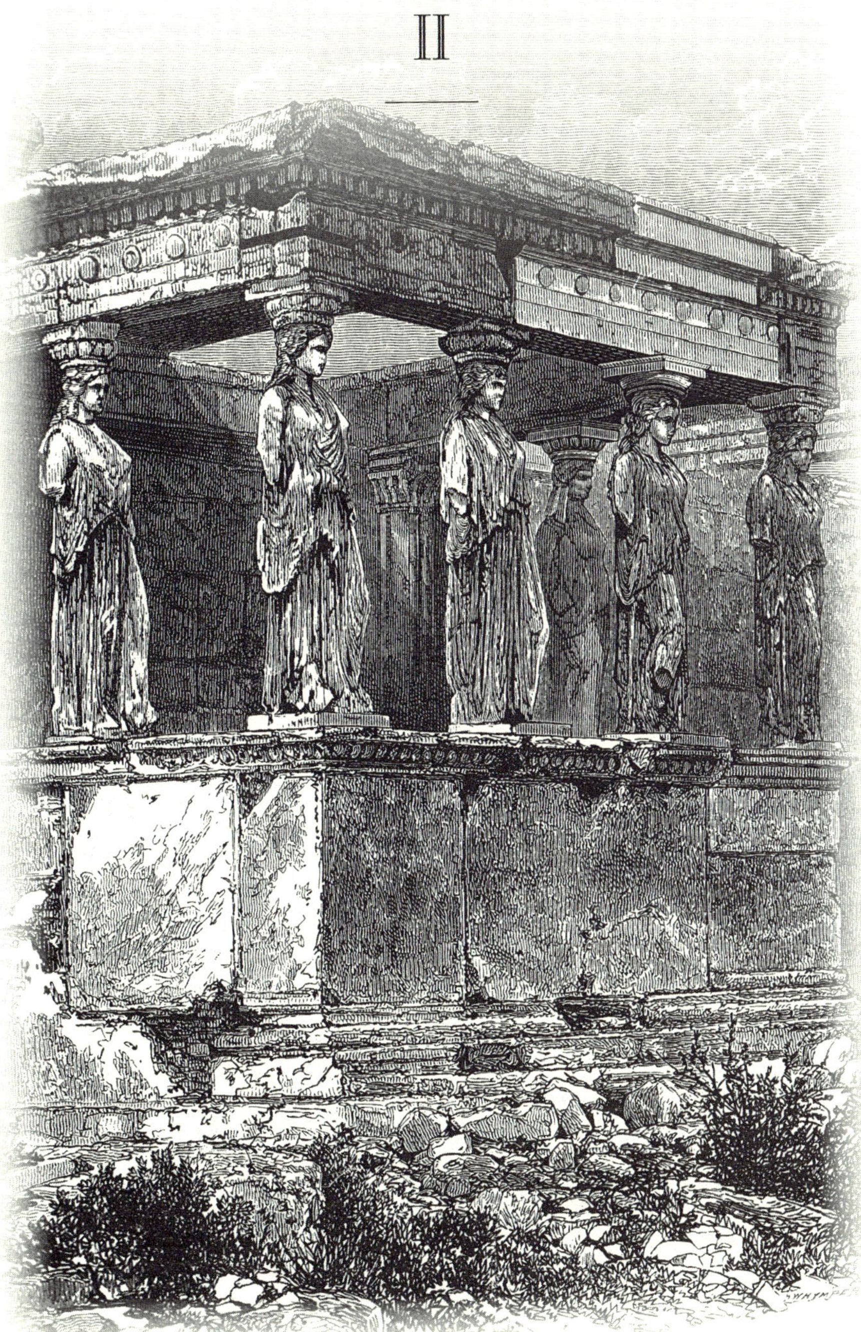

How do you start a poem? Well, the same way you start a building … you dig a hole deep enough to support it.

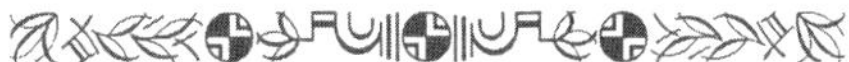

Variation on Frost: the poem knows how the ice cube on the table tries to stay cold by being itself.

I can't seem to keep my poems from sounding full of themselves. Whoever is writing this stuff needs to get the shit kicked out of him.

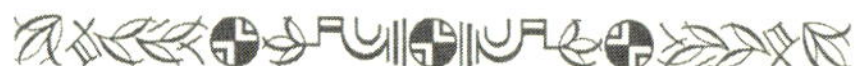

How just once it would be great if one could sneak up on one's own poems, that is, read them as though for the first time, as though they were written by someone else, as though they were recognizable news. That question we ask of another's work with casual indifference, 'Is this any good?' and have no trouble answering.

Poetry may be the one genre where one can, and perhaps ought to, feel like a foreign-language speaker. The ear reaching after scraps of sense.

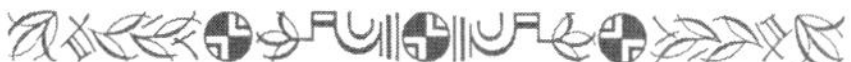

At a lighthouse. There are two ways of communicating with ships at sea: a beam of light or a foghorn. You need the foghorn, naturally, for when there is heavy fog, when you cannot see. Sound cuts through the element that cannot be looked through. I'm just thinking about how poems 'get across'.

Poetry is like the penny: its value is primary and makes everything possible. We just don't carry it any longer in our pockets.

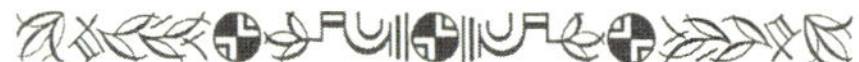

If you only look at a poem's shape, like a painting, you miss hearing it. If you listen to it at a reading, like a piece of music, you miss apprehending it. Is there an equivalent to this in the other art forms? As you listen to a piece of music, there is little sense that you are getting only one part of the experience, where you think, oh, I'd like to see this written down (well, okay, musicians do this ...). Or where you think of staring at a painting as only one part of the experience. This sense that the poem slips through the cracks of time and space.

Poem as a problem-solving exercise. You fiddle about like a mathematician with some unfinished equation and with the addition of an unexpected floating variable find yourself staring into the face of God.

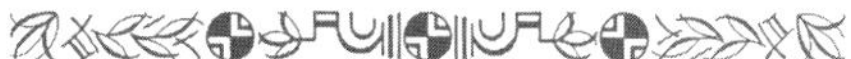

How poems ought to end. The work of finding little windows or avenues of expansion expressed in the very language of conclusion.

Coming to the end of a poem you are writing is like solving a Rubik's cube. You gradually get more and more of the parts lined up. As you get closer to finishing there is a narrowing of possible moves; they cannot be advanced without shifting or spoiling configurations already in place, whose solutions have sped you to that point. The way you've put it together so far has made it impossible to solve it further. You must retreat, unmake the tempting patterns, and try again. Sometimes we cheat and repaint one or two of the sides to make it look finished. Or worse, we publish our poems as half-solved Rubik's cubes.

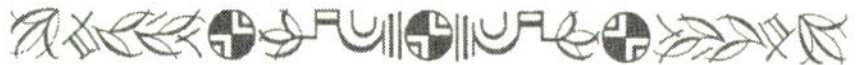

This metaphor stuff is so much in the air. Zwicky is well ahead of me—and yet I believe that, if there is a zeitgeist of ideas, then we are merely conduits for it. Something is trying to get itself said through us and our job is to get in the way as little as possible. I always get in the way.

The strangeness of metaphor is that you start to see it everywhere, which means that it is also nowhere. We say the same thing of God.

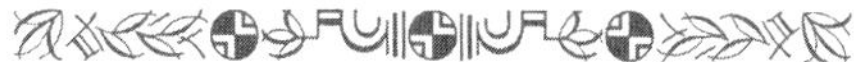

Writing the metaphor book: the illusion of having assembled a picture puzzle, when all you did was paint a picture over blank pieces already locked together.

I keep coming back to this idea that our earliest habits of metaphoric thinking represented metaphoric thinking in its purest form. In a descriptive age like our own, metaphor is always downgraded to its decorative or manipulative status, quite actually beside the point. Early homo sapiens would hear thunder and say to themselves, 'The god Thor is angry.' Thunder identified with a presence. We come along later and say, 'Ah my friend, that's a charming identification, but it is only a metaphor.' They say, 'No, that *was* the god Thor.' We condescend to those thinkers, but we do the same thing. Mary calls John down to supper. She says, 'John, supper is ready.' John says to himself, 'That's Mary calling me down to supper.' He makes a confident identification of certain sound patterns and voice timbre with some idea he has of Mary and dinners. He only licenses the identification because he feels that the words point to something that is actually so. That is only what his forebears were doing. In both there is the necessary identification of word with presence. In a descriptive age, we simply have different rules for what licenses the leap across the gap, but we still make it on faith.

That A = B is a paradox, that a thing is not what it is, is a window onto the further reality it disguises.

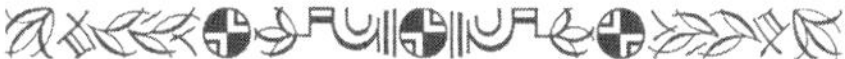

Metaphor would appear to be like the bodhisattvas in Mahayana Buddhism, a towards-which, an agent that is still a part of our language in this world, but whose looked-forward-to erasure of subject and object renders itself unnecessary at its limit. It stays 'on this side' of language, as it were, in order to teach the path that leads beyond it. It leads by erasing itself and not erasing itself.

Dismissers of metaphor complain, 'Sure, this is *like* that, but are they *related*?' The defence rests, Your Honour.

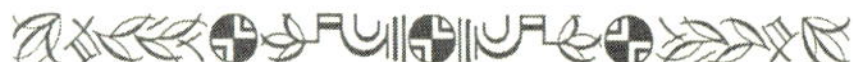

In the end, reason cannot save a society. It has got to be based on some form of metaphoric identification, an 'I am you', or it will come to a chaos of solitudes.

When you say, 'You are me', you steal something from the other. When you say, 'We are one', you still steal something from the other. When you say, 'I am you', you steal something from both. But it is more generous. No one becomes anyone else, but as a gesture, as an imaginative possibility, 'I am you' attempts an evacuation of the ego, and waits.

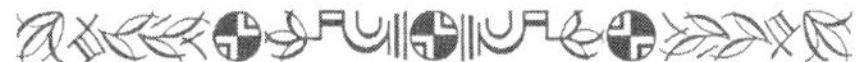

Metaphor out in the world, employed moment to moment, instant to instant. It is a kind of social synapse. Metaphor is to culture what the synapse is to the brain. Cultures of course are brains writ large.

In one sense, the poem has no power itself to bridge the gap between word and thing. But that gap, seen aright in the poem, is an illusion. Once one sees as much, the poem, any poem, becomes existential in that it embodies and exercises the very stuff of the real as we know it. If the illusion is not recognized, then the gap looms and severs. There are things and there are words about things. No amount of talking about bridges can bridge the gap. But the poem invites us to consider that the gap *is* a bridge. Stevens' old pun about aboutness: 'Just things about,' he says.

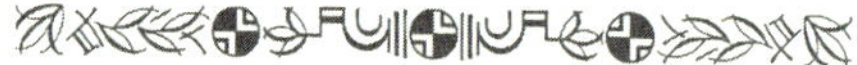

Once literature is seen as an evolved extension of physical reality, it becomes an especially intense and exemplary rearrangement of the world's furniture. It is no longer a man making a drawing about what a room would look like if the furniture were arranged thus, but a man actually moving the couch and table around, standing back and saying, 'What do you think?' There is still an element of hypothesis—we don't have to leave things this way—but the couch makes an actual scraping sound when you drag it across the floor.

Metaphor and nothingness. A = B ➛ C. The arrow is the resonance that flows from the linking of A and B. It is the unknowable, the uncanny at the heart of metaphor. It is actually a part of the equal sign, for the equal sign itself is a vector: a between-where moving elsewhere. Nothingness as charged with potential energy.

There are existential implications. Death is the vector beyond, but also the unknowable thing among us, the gap, the between-where that is elsewhere. So with metaphor: the resonance of a thing-not and the nothing-beyond that the resonance also is. I should learn to smoke pot.

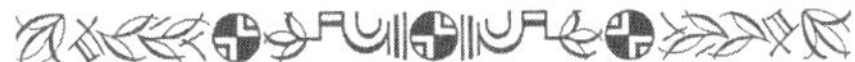

Metaphor and its dimensions of meaning recall the problem of there being in string theory more dimensions than we can see. When you say A = B, you create a further dimension of meaning—we also call it a world—that can't be accommodated to the one you know. It is a hypothetical world made out of related parts in the observable world. Perhaps this is the way to think about dimensions in string theory. We try to imagine another dimension in which the metaphor is literally (scientists would say 'mathematically') true.

String theory derives from an incongruence and tries to move past it towards a mathematical unity, which then drives the production of multiple dimensions. A poem, says Frye, derives from a 'block' in experience. It tries to move past it by creating an alternative picture of what the world 'is like' that makes sense. That world too is multiple according to the dimensions of reading that are embedded in the metaphors. Bishop writes, 'I caught a tremendous fish', and we say it must be so, it all makes sense, but it beggars belief.

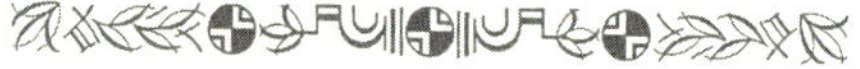

Each new theory in physics (ex. string theory) pushes us in a different direction in the field of metaphoric thinking. We go from 'is and is not' in quantum mechanics to extra-metaphoric worlds in the dimensions of string theory. The final unification theory is unification theory itself: metaphor.

Blake's guinea-sun 'experiment' is the quantum physicist's double-slit experiment, but with different conclusions drawn.

Questioner to Blake: 'What, when you look with your naked eye, do you not see the sun as it actually is?' Blake: 'No no no, I see only the visionary sun, the heavenly host singing "Holy Holy Holy is the Lord God Almighty." I look *through* the physical world, not *with* it.'

Questioner to Physicist: 'What, when you look at the electrons, do you not see them as they actually behave?' Physicist: 'No, I see only a paradox, something otherworldly and mysterious. If I could look *through* the material world, rather than *with* it, I would see what was really there.'

Neil deGrasse Tyson saying that math is the language of the universe. Depends on what he means. Certainly, mathematicians write poems of a sort, make identifications and leaps, adapt parts to wholes. No end of beauty. But the language they use is a system of measurement, of quantities. It does not name a thing into being. Whereas *language* language is primarily ontological. It measures nothing. The mathematician says 'This is this much.' The poet says 'This is.' Math is content and plot, but not being.

The mathematician might answer, 'No, the number 1 points to the being of a single thing.' The poet replies, 'No, you take the object's being for granted and tell us how many of it there are.' Like the god of Genesis who names things into being (for instance, 'Let there be one-ness'), the poet speaks the number 1 to invoke the possibility of the existence of a single thing, the number 2 to evoke the possibility of the existence of two things, and so on. Such a 'one thing' can now be, because we have made a name for it. 'Tree' is the name for the brown and green thing outside and says that it is. Again, the mathematician must take this for granted, which is why words are demoted. So deGrasse Tyson merely skipped a step. Math is the language of the universe only because language is the language of the universe.

I've been trying out a new metaphor with physicists: gravity is a form of time travel. Follow and be cheerful. Gravity warps the fabric of space-time towards the centre of a large mass like the earth. For someone at that centre, time moves (by small fractions) more slowly relative to the person on the surface of the earth. A person at the centre of the earth would be in my past. I am pulled towards the past because the past isn't finished yet. How could it be otherwise? We fall in the direction of our childhoods, if only a little way.

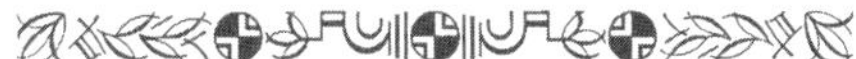

Every clicked-on link on a web page is like a new pertinence in metaphor. You see an associative link between where you are and where you might be and you 'activate' the relationship by moving from the first to the second. The link is a synecdoche (a part of the whole on the first page links you to the second), but also metonymy, because it is 'put for' the new possibility beyond it. It may be part of why we get addicted to surfing the web: worlds expanding metaphorically. The difference of course is that in genuine metaphoric thinking, no one has decided beforehand what page you will land on when you make the leap.

The place of metaphoric thinking in the age of digital media. Web pages are like so many tenors and vehicles. Their links are a series of associated commonplaces. Each tenor was formerly a vehicle, each vehicle becomes a tenor. The leap between. Every bookmark is a dead metaphor.

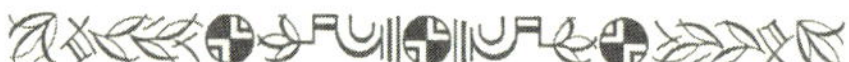

Someone needs to discover a way of sending energy or electricity via a signal. It would be the ultimate material equivalent of a metaphor, and it would of course change everything.

Cosmology as a problem at Tim Hortons. No one here forgets his lines. No one is nervous, waiting in turn. No more rehearsals. All is natural, spontaneous. Not a line dropped, not a step or gesture mistaken. 'Bacon breakfast sandwich, please, on a homestyle, no cheese.' How perfectly the cup falls to the floor from the child's hand and splashes. The props crew, they all think they're poets.

III

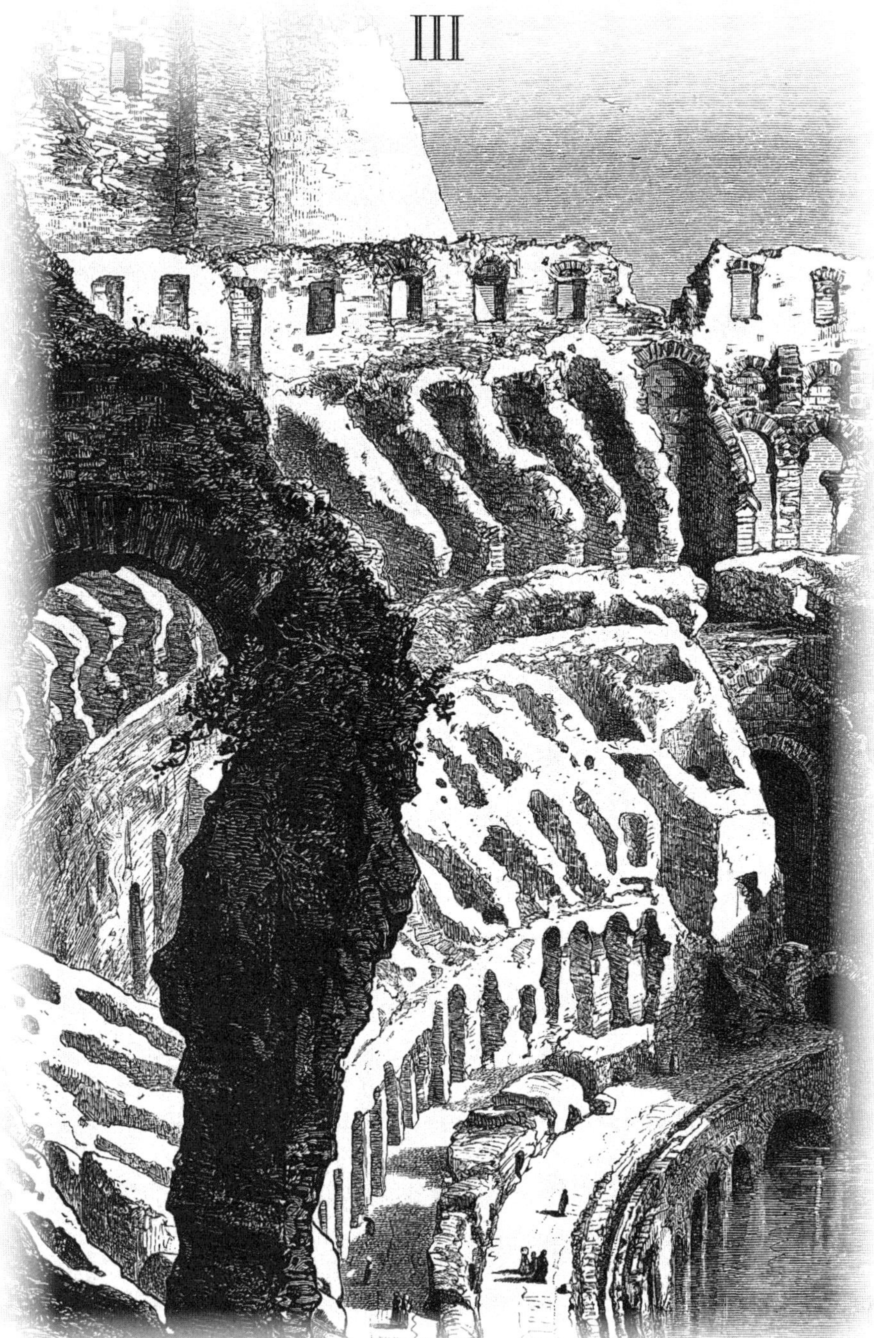

I'm not sure that I read poems for pleasure. But I do remember them for pleasure.

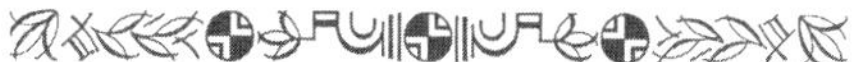

My damnable slow reading. I finish a book and it's like winning a victory over it. I throw it down on the floor and fire three bullets into it for good measure.

With all their scratches and ticks, LPs are a record of their having been listened to. Books with their stretched bindings and scribbles are a record of their having been read. Seems not to be as true of paintings. A painting is not worn down by our looking at it. Though it does become a record, as all these media are, of the time it has endured.

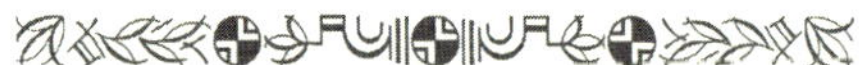

Everything we write should be in parentheses. History will add them, in any case.

Readers are lawyers. The text is the matter at hand. It is also the judge.

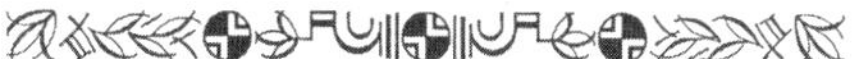

This idea that one has in one's head a Wallace Stevens space, an Elizabeth Bishop space. That you can summon to mind the feeling, the idea, the *state of being*, invoked by a certain poet, just by speaking the name. One says, for instance, Auden, and without your recalling any particular Auden line, an Audenesque world rises to attention. True of course for music and painting as well. A sign of the artist's ultimate success.

Christian Bök's DNA experiment is quite like, at least no better than, George Herbert's seventeenth-century acrostics, in a poem such as 'Jesu', where you find a code written inside a word or phrase and then look to see what that code itself might 'write out' when given leave. The unseen spirit in Herbert, the unseen genome in Bök. In both the sense of a secret wellspring at the heart of the poem, brought to life, actualized. *Tout ça change, tout c'est la meme chose.*

In his biography of William Cowper, Neil Currie uses the denigrating term 'echo-location' for the pointless work of merely identifying echoes, as though echo-location were merely synonymous with echo-spotting. But he neglects to listen for the original meaning of the phrase: to find one's way via sonar and its echoes. Poets are the blind bats who see their way through the dark by echo-location. They bounce a phrase of their own off a corresponding phrase in the literature around them and find their bearings in relation to the reverberations that come back to them. The critic's mere location of echoes is pushed further by the poet's echo-location.

Echo-location. The poet-bat finding her way in the dark. Does she project her voice into the written world or into the world of things, listening for 'feedback'? Both, evidently. The written world is certainly part of the world of things, if not the whole part.

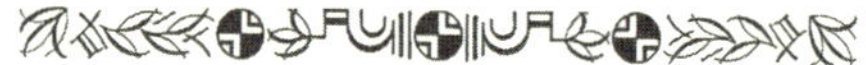

Frye's so-called critical system (I think 'vision' is a better word) has a kind of metaphoric relation to the material it purports to describe, as do all systems. People sometimes balk at it because they feel it is something too complete, too fixed in its metrics and patterns. But it is an imaginative cosmology like any great fiction—Dante, Blake—that half creates and half perceives its subject. Quantum physicists know this.

Reading Benjamin's 'The Work of Art in the Age of Mechanical Reproduction' and his critique of the aura, which surprised me as I'd always thought the term was a positive one in his work. I thought it meant the thing that is lost when you look at a reproduction of a painting rather than at the painting itself, the 'right thereness' of the thing looked at. But he argues that the aura reifies and stabilizes the structures of authority in a culture, fetishizing the object and so on. Reproductions of art on the other hand can transgress their auras, challenging prevailing social movements in art, and thereby social movements generally. Of course Benjamin didn't live to see the age of the Iphone snapshot and the selfie. He might now be talking about the authenticity of the uncheapened, unphotoshopped Bonnard in the Musée. He might be crying out, 'Please! Give me an image with an aura!'

It is the same demonization of the imaginative work that we find in literary criticism among ideological readers: the work disguises and propagates structures of authority because it is given over, *and* transparent, to them. But the work is also transparent to other revolutionary initiatives that lie at its heart. The ideological and imaginative are set against one another in a work. It isn't a question of demonizing the work, 'interrogating' it under bright lights until it confesses, but of seeing how it is the place where human being struggles with and against its own worst habits, trying to release itself from where it is, into a world that may be. This is the same process that Benjamin himself advocates in his celebration of cinema. Cinema trains the audience in a 'plasticity of perspective'. As Benjamin himself had been accused of over-prizing film in the same way that he sees pre-industrial art as over-prizing the original artwork and its aura, he might have been more sensitive to the tension. In the end, as a writer, I think he was.

The scientists end up facing the same crisis we do in literary studies. Our ideological criticism—where we are essentially automatons mouthing the axioms of our culture—anticipates their anxiety regarding free will, where, as Mary Midgley says, 'One's ideas have been inserted into one by a Svengali.'

Our jargons in the disciplines of English can be awfully embarrassing, especially when they are used merely to sound as though they mean something. We deserve all the parodies of our style that are out there. On the other hand, we make great allowances for all the abstruseness and opacity of scientific formulas and descriptions. We assume that the scientists know what they are talking about and are off doing their thing. They'll let us know the upshot when the time comes. Why not grant the same allowances to humanists? There is a form of condescension in those who quote an opaque passage of literary theory that literary criticism should never be hard to grasp, should not possess a kind of shorthand for the work it takes up, and should always speak so that someone outside the discipline could understand it. It would be like making fun of a quantum physicist when he quotes the wave function formula, jeering at him for not speaking in a language that dogs and cats can understand. At the same time (humanists take note ...), few quantum physicists quote the wave function formula just to sound like someone who knows how to quote the wave function formula. At least (he says sitting in a plane at 35,000 feet), I certainly hope not.

Teaching large classes as a kind of orchestra rehearsal. You are the conductor. The poem on the screen is the score. The students are the players. You raise your baton. You work on particular parts of the score, drawing out certain players, certain sections of instruments, going over them, testing levels and intonations, assimilating instruments to one another, drawing this utterance to the fore, letting another serve as complement. A whole gradually assembling. And of course there is no actual performance. Only the sense that we are ready now.

IV

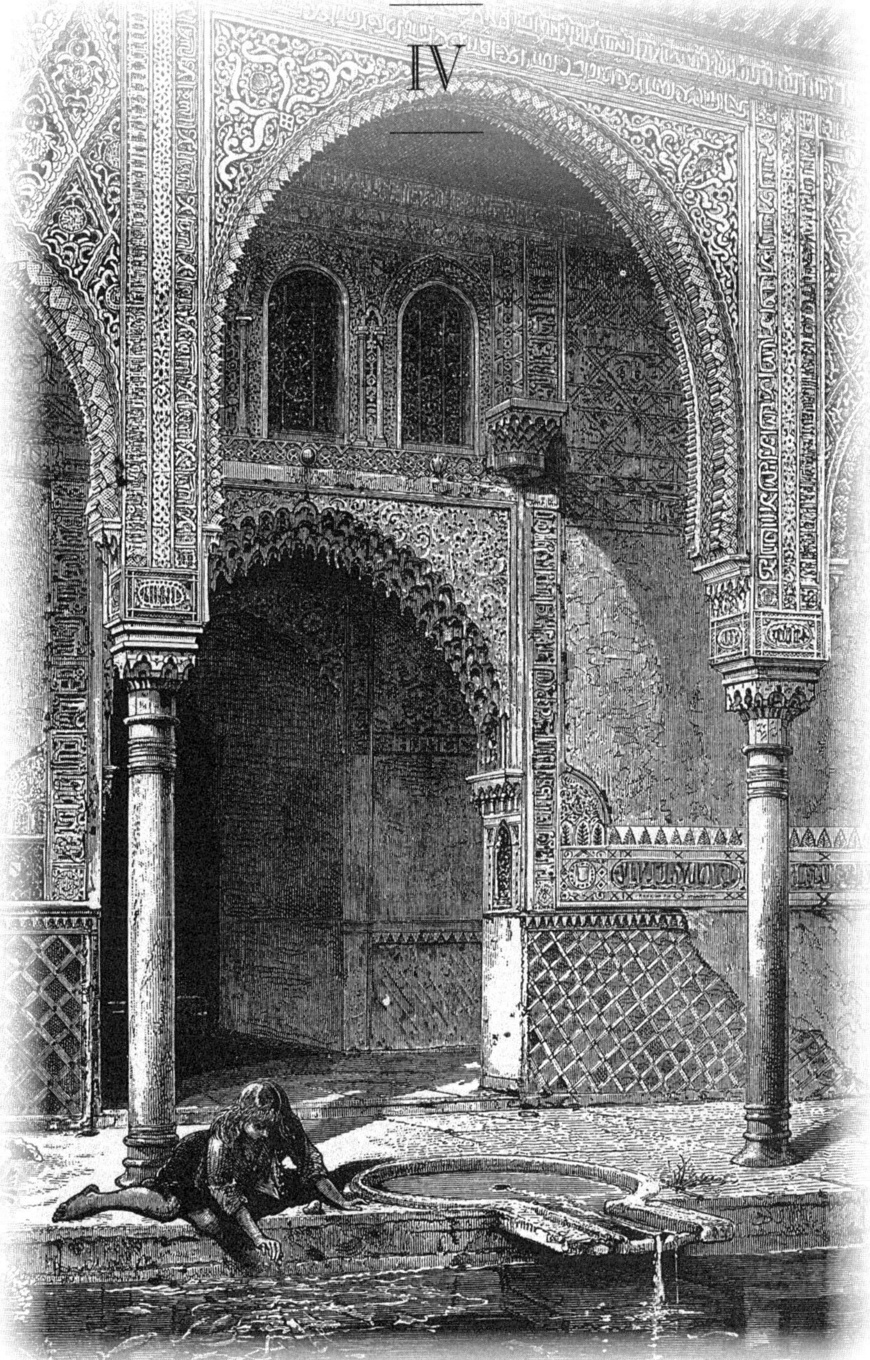

We go about our lives doing an infinitesimal fraction of what we might. Look at us. We think we have all the time in the world. If we really understood that our lives hung by a thread (Jonathan Edwards, anyone?), our potential in every living moment would be infinite. The irony of the fact that if we really knew we were going to die, we would become gods.

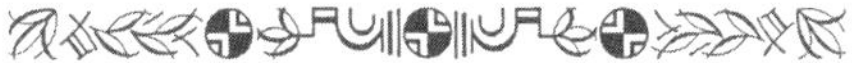

I believe in God. I just don't think he exists yet. Why do we let ourselves say this of peace, but not of God? Is it the capital letter?

God is like a bubble under water. Not something you can burst with a pin, hard as you try. You can only move it around until you let it rise to the top of its element, at which point there is nothing there but a clarity for it to burst into, which of course is what it contained within itself all along.

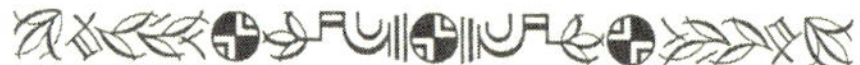

Spirit is to organized religion
as literature is to ideology.

Revelation and prophecy, that old Show and Tell.

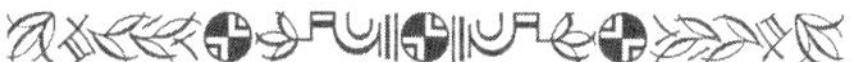

We speak of spirit in the same way that a blind man takes photographs with a camera.

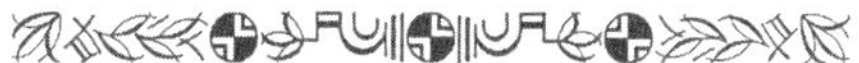

We hope for a time when we will no longer need to hope. We only need to hope when we are alive.

The emptiness or pointlessness you can feel performing a ritual is appropriate in a sense. A priest puts a cookie in the mouth of an adherent: she feels nothing, possibly even a slight embarrassment. I suppose the idea is that a meaning has been offloaded from her *into* the ritual. She is *bound* to feel empty. The ritual allows her to feel empty; that is its privilege. We often think of rituals as inspiring a devotion, calling it up each time. But there is this other sense too of the ritual absorbing a meaning you can no longer sustain. This may be why rituals seem more important to us as we age. We trust that, however weary we are of the effort, the ritual contains, and performs, how we might feel for it.

Of course, this may just be an excuse for how rituals become unthinking, rote, and so potentially dangerous. Goebbels was performing a ritual with a trite wave of his hand dividing the new trainload of Jews into those who would live and those who would not. Book burnings are a form of cult ritual. But there is a dissociation from the objects ritualized, where it is actually the ritual behaviour and its repetitiveness that dulls the reality of what you are doing. A dangerous ritual says, 'Let me protect you by disguising the meaning of what you are doing.' A hopeful ritual says, 'Let me hold what you have done until you are ready to feel for it again.'

A dangerous ritual is a wastebasket. You have the dissociation. You both perform and discard the performance. A hopeful ritual is a … what? A soil perhaps. You plant a seed, see nothing there, and wait.

I keep coming back to my favourite Stevens adage: 'The final belief is to believe in a fiction which you know to be a fiction, there being nothing else; the exquisite truth is to know that it is a fiction and that you believe in it willingly.' The idea requires a more careful defence in the age of 'fake news'. There are those political extremists—the 'tin hat' types—who seem to believe in their particular group's fantasies. They're disqualified because they actually believe them as truths, which isn't of course what Stevens meant. You must *know* they are fictions. But there are also plenty of extremists in politics, sinister types past and present, who are perfectly aware that their fictions are fictions and know how to trade with them, in their scrimmage for power, in the great marketplace of lies. But again, they don't promote them *as* fictions. The current president would say, 'this report is fake news', but he would never say, 'I know this report isn't really fake news but I'm going to say so and believe in my saying so as a fiction, because that is my right.' What Frye called the 'excluded initiative' at the heart of ideological language must be imaginative language itself. The politician wants to use fictions but doesn't want you thinking that they *are* fictions.

So we simply come back to the same principle as applied to rituals. The book-burner detaches himself from the books he is ritually burning. He doesn't jump into the fire with them. What the president-liar dissociates himself from, with his ritual morning tweets, is the public itself that is the ultimate object of his ritual lies. The citizenry itself becomes the pile of dangerous books that the book-burner must burn.

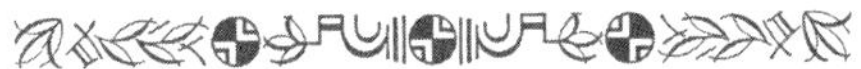

It reminds me of an ambiguity at the heart of the term 'make-believe' that makes for special trouble in our understanding of literature and ideology. Where make-believe is concerned, you can't, and shouldn't try to, 'make another believe'. It is only your own relationship to the imaginative act that you can control. This goes for the author as much as for any religious adherent. Make-believe asks you to understand that you make what you believe, and only then does it become a special way of believing in what you make.

Faith *in*. The conventional meaning suggests a thinking towards the thing believed in. One believes *in* God. What a strange preposition. As though you were climbing into the box of what you believe. But that's too rigid. There is Frye's idea that faith is the effort to make real what one has faith in. Faith *in* comes to mean a faith that constitutes the imagined object of faith and so resides within it. This is more than just saying that faith in a god *is* that god. There is the added sense that the thinking you do, or have managed at any one point, is the expression-limit of what you have faith in, but not its exhaustion. Related to Ricoeur's idea that metaphor is an exhortation to 'think more'.

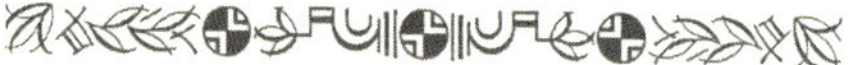

And everyone embodies this kind of faith, the web scammer as much as the bodhisattva. You get up in the morning and you pull on a pair of socks. You head to work. You're meeting a friend. You behave inside a set of intentions which, according to your behaviour, are gradually embodied. Whatever your day became, that was the god you were, in the process of things, effectively realizing. The cabinetmaker builds a cabinet, turns out the light, and closes the door.

There is a becomingness that passes through us.

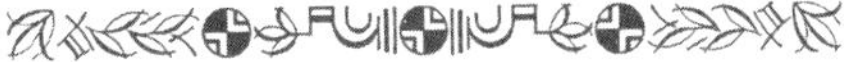

An answer for the non-sequential structure of the Qur'an and its penchant for repetition: 'If there has been drought, you do not complain that one drop is the same as the other.'

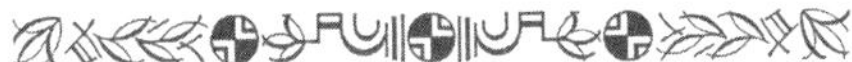

The Qur'an seems to align predominantly with the Book of Revelation, hence its emphasis on apocalyptic battle and a final separation of the good from the infidel. It is the final trial in all romance narratives, their worlds dividing into the damned and the elect. The Bible likes to fill in the backstory, but the Qur'an cuts to the chase.

This business of the outdated mythology. We point to some of the stricter attitudes towards women in Christianity and Islam as proof that the religions have been outgrown, if they haven't actually failed. No errors are permitted. But in science we excuse Hiroshima as an unfortunate consequence that has to be understood in its total historical context. In Richard Dawkins's universe, science can look past its controversial outcomes—pollution, destruction—as unfortunate side effects, because it is fighting the good fight, as he sees it, and trying to improve. Religions on the other hand are just dangerous. Science gets to be held harmless, thought of as a process trying to work itself out; religious thinking does not. No wonder Dawkins doesn't like to think of science as the new religion.

Why is it that religious adherents don't like to think of their central writings as works in progress? Because their god wrote them, and gods only write perfect works? Why couldn't a god write a 'perfect' work that was also a work in progress? Why couldn't the fact that a work was in progress be part of what makes it perfect?

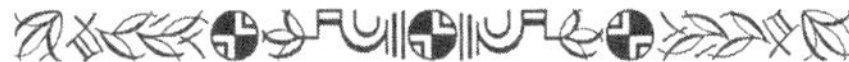

Defenders keep trying to put a god at the beginning of the evolutionary process. It makes more sense to put a god at the end of the evolutionary process, the allowing conditions towards which we evolve in order to find out what it may be.

The status of the miracle in religious and scientific thinking. Religion says there are things that cannot be explained in physical terms: they are miracles and transgress the laws of cause and effect. The scientists say that there are no gaps in cause and effect, therefore no miracles. We may not understand all the laws of physics, but whatever they are, they observe themselves and do not violate their own charter. The disagreement then is over the meaning of the gap itself between cause and effect, which is a disagreement over the nature of metaphoric relation that breathes there.

We are as mystified in the sciences by the nature of mind and consciousness as we used to be by the nature of God. The mysteries of cognition are probably just the next evolutionary expression, now in secular terms, of the problem 'I am that I am.' The cognitive philosophers have become the new priests and shamans, where the original priests and shamans were the first cognitive philosophers.

V

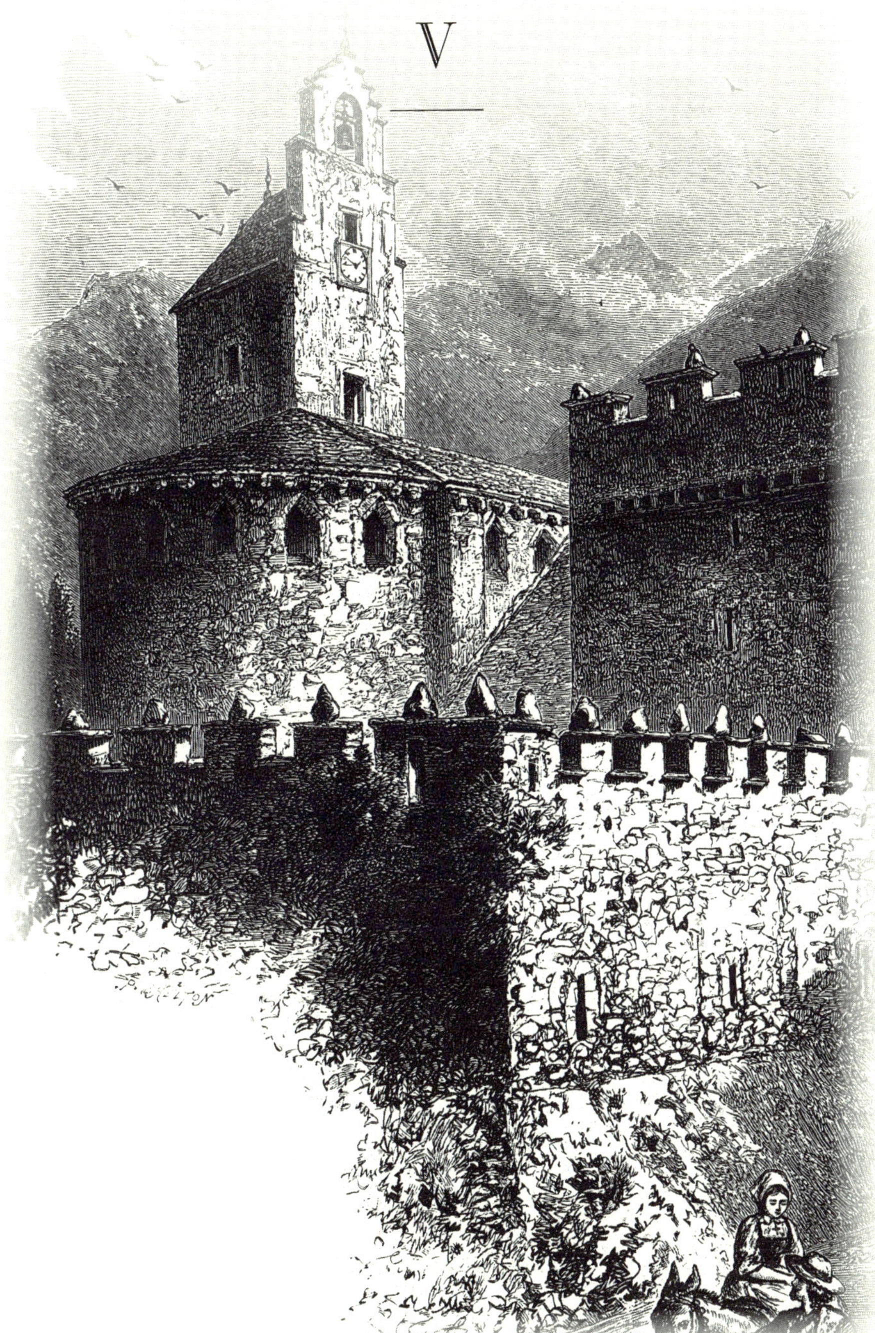

The nervous system cannot experience the world. It can only experience itself. Not a tree, but what the nervous system has to say about itself when it encounters a tree. Alice B. Toklas saying that whenever Gertrude Stein walked into the room she heard a little bell chime in her mind.

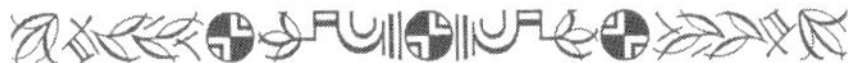

We ask, does a plant have consciousness? We get closer to the mystery when we ask, how does your forearm feel about being a forearm? There it is right there, alive and well. How does it feel about being itself? Or even, how does your brain (not your mind, mind, but your brain) feel about being a brain?

Richard Wilbur's 'Mind' gets at the essential strangeness of consciousness. The inside of the brain must be pitch-black. Yet thoughts find their way around in that darkness, and in this darkness we see light. It is like the photograph of a sunny day printed in the middle of a closed book.

Actual consciousness may be like the observed scene of a dream, where thinking the image *is* seeing it. Or rather, you generate the image and 'see it' at the same time. I like the idea that the illusion of consciousness is a form of dream, at once a making and a having.

My sense of self—the feeling of consciousness as a 'happening to oneself'—is the moisture that rises from the boiling pot, a product of the body's heat. A misty vapour is freed from its material source by the heat applied to it. Once the heat is removed, the vapour must settle back into the grosser substance whence it arose. Our usual metaphor for this is a body returning to earth, to its material source, except here it is the mind that returns to its element. The body is the mind's earth.

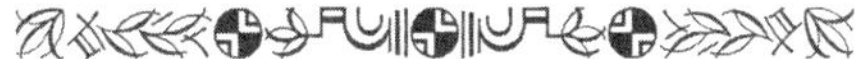

Paradox of the fact that the ipseity of another (his or her ownhood ...) is both impossible to imagine and simply what one feels oneself. The radical of existential metaphor. I have no idea what it feels like to be you. But I know for certain that it is exactly the same as what it feels like to be me. How do you do.

Personality is what rolls off the great assembly line of conscious illusion: our being able to live (whatever the facts) *as though* we were more than chemicals in a jar. It is the great innocence, the one we are grounded in, lose as we age, and must find a way back to, credulous *and* tongue-in-cheek.

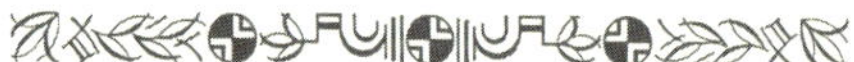

Try out the idea that consciousness is an illusion, but where the illusion has a certain reality. What happens to the 'being as' or the 'seeming so' when its material conditions dissipate and return to earth? It does not, as itself, simply head off to 'join' some other combination of elements to become *its* 'seeming as'. The 'seeming as' is not transferable, even if the chemicals are. And yet there is the sense still that oblivion is unstable because it is made up of elements that are always changing. It may then be a question of the 'seeming as' remaining always still potential, if forever after not quite expressed in the same way. The afterlife as merely an instability at the heart of nothingness. We take what we can get.

Consciousness and self-justification. To have a thought is to feel that that is the thought to have. We grant it to ourselves, but rarely to others.

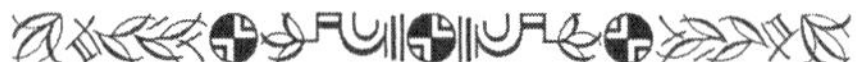

I try to keep my narcissism to myself.

Frye saying that no one was ever convinced by an argument. I think of all the ideological differences between the Left and the Right nowadays, how we talk past one another, prefer our own echo chambers and so on. Why do we not like to be wrong? It is an odd experience indeed to be shown that the thoughts just now happening to you are the wrong thoughts. It is almost impossible to dissociate your own being-conscious with the thoughts that populate it. They feel like the same thing: cognitive experience that *occurs* to you. To be told that you are wrong, then, is to be told that you have the wrong kind of consciousness, which is absurd. We find ourselves in the odd position of trying to defend the rightness of something that simply is. Pope's 'Whatever is, is right' goes to this. He's wrong of course. But we have to meet him half-way. Whatever we *think* is *feels* right.

Much depends of course on being able to listen to one's own cognitive dissonance, how one thought not quite fitting with another is the crack that lets the light in. To think metaphorically, to associate your consciousness not with its particular contents at any given moment, but with its ability to be what it is, a connection generator, a *thinking more*. This amounts to letting your consciousness be a consciousness, a reaching after its own state. To think, as your mind wanders and comes to a block in the road, 'Thank God. And I thought I was lost!'

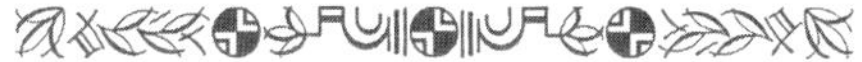

This thing that I hardly dare admit to myself that everything seems less and less real to me. That what is happening is not really happening … and my associating this with a kind of depression. My not being able to wake up inside how what is happening is happening. But along with it, the increasing sense that it is only in words that things have any reality at all. Writing out 'Everything is less and less real to me' becomes a kind of living fossil, real in its own right.

I've always felt that my main job in life was to be that random person you see walking towards you on the city sidewalk. All the people you see around you: man waiting in a car, person at bus stop, person turning into your aisle at the grocery store. Where do they find us all? What if they run out of people? Each of us is trying to make up the difference. Not how I got here, where I'm going and what I hope for, not what it's like to be inside me at this moment. Just: I can be that man who is the sort of man you are likely to see crossing the street when I cross the street, if I hurry.

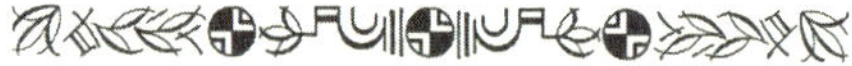

There cannot, must not, be a competition of inwardnesses among us as we pass in the street. We will either die ashamed of ourselves or knock each other down.

In the social macrocosm, if books were brain cells then we physical readers would be the synapses that connect them. And all the world would be thinking.

Each of us inside a kind of enforced solipsism. You sit around a table at a meeting. You see that everyone there has his or her own perspective on what we each imagine is a kind of total picture, called perhaps 'This moment of our being seated around a table.' We think the moment exists, beyond our own imagining of it. But it is only a hypothesis, perhaps even an illusion. I look around the room and think of what it must look like to each of the others, from their physical angle, and from within their minds, with me here sitting over at one end, being an example of the sort of person you might find sitting around a table at a meeting. There is no *between* each of our perspectives, though we imagine that betweenness as filled with our all being here. We used to imagine, as a kind of comfort, that the reality of our sitting here around a table was registered in something like the mind of God, a total imagination that contains the presence of the whole scene. A quiet but reassuring, 'Yes, this moment is what it is.' Apparently the imagination does the work anyway, for here we are, sitting around a table.

Think of this analogy. There is a room called 'All of us sitting here at the table' and you are outside it, in a separate cell with a little slot for passing notes back into the room. Each thing you say and do is a message that is passed into the room to relay what you have said and done. Messages return from the room, of what you see, hear, smell, etc. The sustained and consistent interplay of messages leaves you feeling that there is such a thing as 'The conversation we are having here.' But this is what everyone else is doing too! They are outside a room, in their own cells, sending in their own messages and getting responses. There is no one in the room itself. The room is empty and dark, and the presence that we call the reality of our having a conversation here does not exist outside our individual faith in it. Yet our faith in it becomes part of the messaging that returns to us, with word of others who share that faith. One of the messages that comes back is that there is a table in front of you and that others are seated around it. The table is a metaphor for an apparently shared belief that we are having a meeting.

The reality that exists outside our individual consciousness is the same reality that exists after we die. To imagine the former is to be able to imagine the latter. The blackness, the emptiness of that nothing is all around us, but look how we move *through* it.

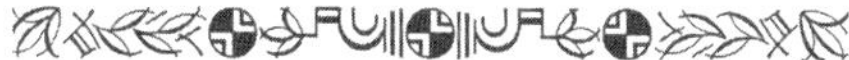

A society can no more pull itself up by its own bootstraps than an individual can choose his own thoughts.

Sam Harris's little book on free will. Awfully repetitive for such a short book. He challenges Daniel Dennett's idea of extending the notion of free will into the unconscious. Harris shows the limitation here. We can't choose our thoughts, he says, any more than we can feel responsible for the fact that we produce red blood cells, etc. We discover what we think. Joyce's 'Thought is the thought of a thought.' Dennett prefers the model of the feedback system, where the conscious mind feeds its products back into the brain's subconscious systems in such a way that a kind of leveraging becomes possible. Harris disputes this but I think he offers something like the same idea turned inside out in social terms. He pictures one conscious individual being in play with the consciousness of every other individual and argues that we must allow this to happen, to unfold, and hope for genuine improvement. Society, instead of the whole brain of the individual, produces the interactions that generate, if not free will, at least unpredictable results. Dennett does the same by folding the mind's conscious thoughts back into the brain's total cognitive activity … and then watching what happens there. In Harris, the possibility of unpredictable relational events (metaphor!) happens not in the mind, but in the world. In Dennett that element of unpredictability is already the gap-enabled metaphoricity of a single mind. In any case, I like this idea that we are each a 'Let's see what happens when someone like me exists in the world.' We are participants in an experiment. Not just observers, but participants. 'What happens when I am this.'

How the ancient oracles go to the current debate over free will. With your every least thought it is as though you had just stepped from the Temple at Delphi. You 'visit' the oracle and ask the following question: 'What is now to be thought?' The delivered message is, 'What occurs to you.' The oracle's answer of course is always ambiguous. What is the meaning, the Sybil teases, of what you have just heard me say? You aren't sure, but you hold the ciphers in your hand. You never doubt, coming from the oracle, that it was meant to be said. 'How do I know what I think until I see what I say,' asked E.M. Forster. This must be the original meaning of the self-fulfilling prophecy. Or course, if you want to find out what the prophecy means, you have to go back to the oracle.

VI

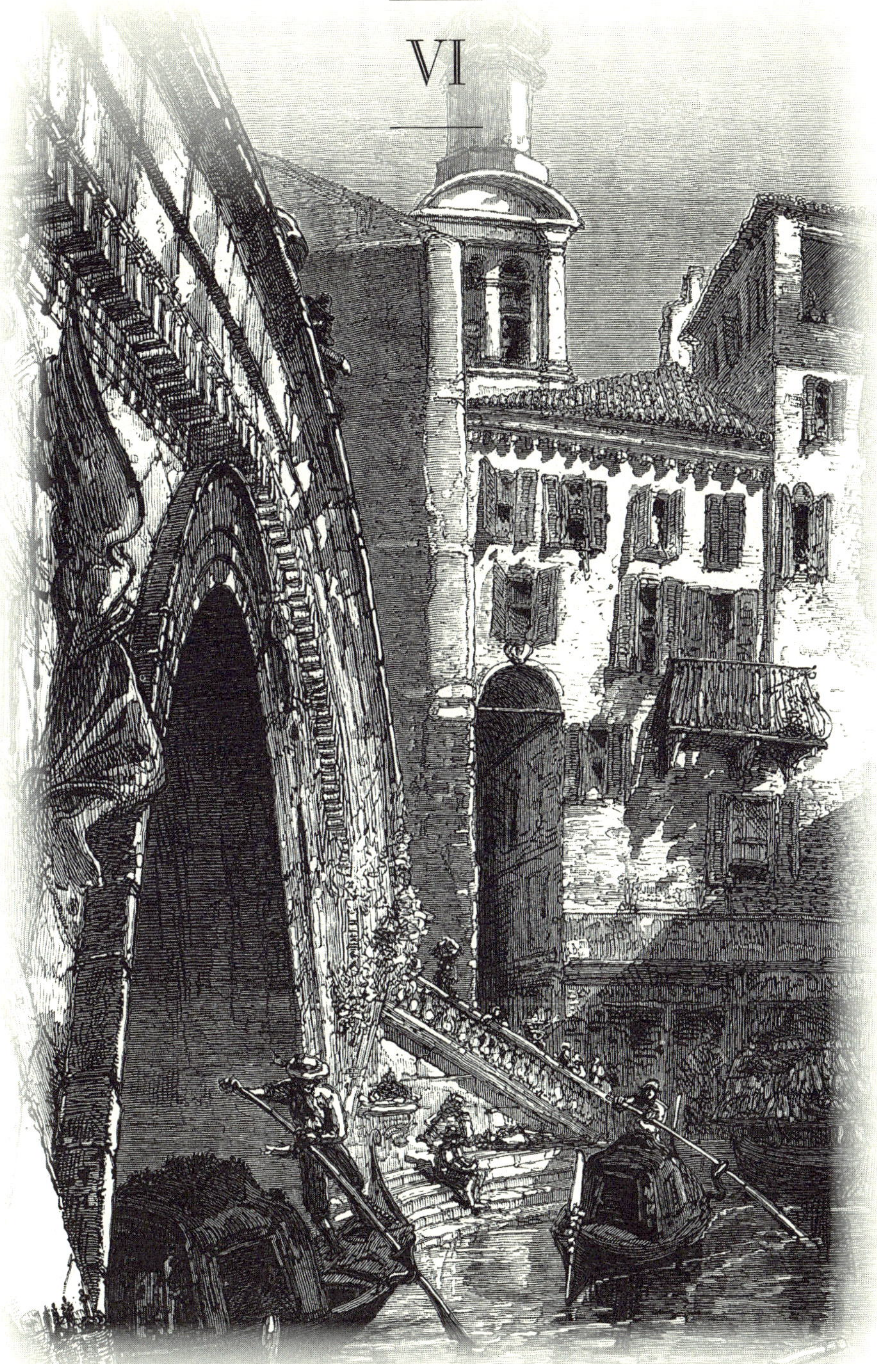

Aging is like taking objects out of a box. It is also like putting objects into a box, packing up. Explains why I don't know if I'm coming or going.

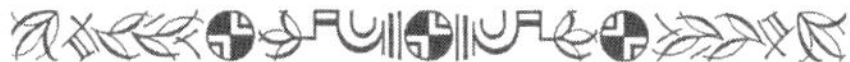

Time appears to be on its own,
but it has many followers.

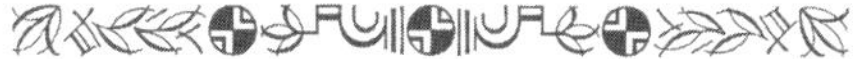

On March 10th the sign advertising the community dance on March 9th is taken down. The mystery of this.

I recall in *Missing Link* that the computational irreducibility of unfolding events makes detailed predictions impossible and that the only way to calculate the outcomes of every instant is to go through them in time. When it comes to events that are *bound* to happen, time itself is the only prognosticator that works.

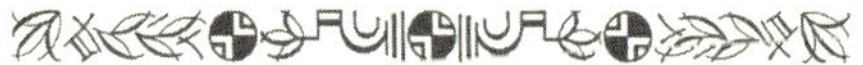

The stories of cause and effect that get told every passing instant are unfinished and incalculable. It's a wonder things figure out how to happen at all.

The present moment: a bit of paper and sticks assembled to make a fire, but where there is no such thing as a match.

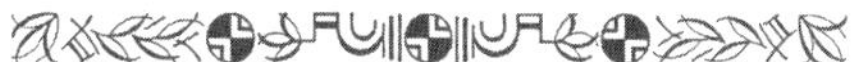

Life is not a window *in* time. It is a window *of* time. With the former, you count the days before it closes. With the latter you no more need to count the days than a soup needs to count up its molecules in order to be soup.

How odd to think of the greats who lived when we did. When I was two years old my parents could have brought me to the actual door of Mr and Mrs T.S. Eliot, and they would have invited us in. Mrs Eliot would have made cootchie faces at me and Tom would have set me on his knee and bounced me up and down and it would have been me there laughing as he did so. And the press would have come with their flashbulbs and Tom, holding me, would have looked obligingly into the cameras with me there in those suspenders I used to wear and the caption in the papers the next day would have read something like 'Prospects Very Disappointing for the New Generation of Poets'. Nothing in physics or in our understanding of time and space would have prevented this from happening if it had happened.

It can only ever be a particular day. Thursday, August 11, 1726, for instance. What must have seemed to recommend that day and that afternoon, for those who stood about in it, was that at the time it was the present moment, and what was more, the latest present moment anyone had known. Simply, a spaciousness.

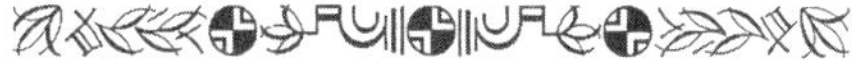

My first recollected image from childhood, hardly even a memory: a light, sepia toned, in the hallway of the Jane Street maisonettes, 1964. It is as though, from the flow of ordinary postcard-minutes, suddenly and for reasons lost to you, one of them drops loose and is addressed and mailed to you in the future. It arrives one day, a postcard in the mail. You look at the image, turn it over, find no greeting, no sender, no explanation, just your name and address standing there, which appear to be correct. A deliverance.

What you want from an early memory is the reality of its being drawn aside. Not the reality of its *having been* drawn aside, but the drawing aside itself. We think of it as a problem of time travel, but really it's a problem of grammatical tense, which is already in our heads.

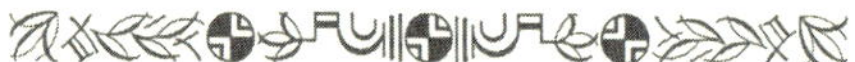

The unreality of memory and our existential ache at its not summoning things past a little better than it does. Anamnesis. I remember getting that word from Auden. The simple act of remembrance, from the original Greek, 'to call back to mind'. But Auden was thinking of the Christian Eucharist and Christ's words, as he breaks and eats the bread, 'Do this in remembrance [anamnesis] of me.' The word 'anamnesis', theologians argue, points to an act of 'communion' that so embodies what it represents that it makes 'here and now effective' what the words say. The summoning act is identified with what it retrieves. It is in the end the mystery of metaphoric thinking and it works the same way for memory itself. Poems look to embody the communion. Marianne Moore, thinking of her deceased mother in the poem 'Faces':

> Certain faces, a few, one or two—or one
> face photographed by recollection—
> to my mind, to my sight,
> must remain a delight.

Over and over, this idea of time being actually a *form* of space. The GI Joe I had when we lived on Dixon Road in the mid-sixties. I would throw it up in the air again and again and let it crash to the ground, mangled. The simple fact that it must lie even now in a landfill site somewhere underneath some well-aged suburban development with its own tall trees and thrice-repaired sewer mains. Even now, it is there, hereabouts somewhere. The idea that time past is like that, still in the same place, still where we are now, just over there in a spot somehow out of sight, buried beneath everything we have done since.

Stevens' moving phrase, 'Farewell my days.' But perhaps we don't leave our days behind. By dying, we stay with them. A form of allegiance, a refusal to go on without them. We don't leave ourselves behind either. What we leave behind is all of time going on ahead.

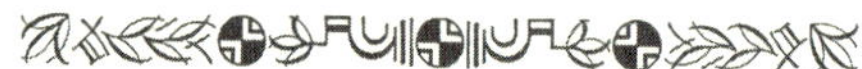

What ultimately is the difference between a timeless heaven and timelessness itself? Probably nothing.

It seems to me that the whole notion of reincarnation is based on this intuition that we are somehow aware of all the time that has passed before we came to be. I feel that fore-time as a strange blank in my 'thinking back'. It is that thought of a nothingness that is incarnated in our not having been there.

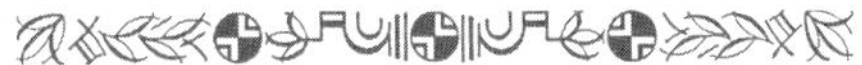

Being alive in this sense then is the opposite of waiting. It is the fact of not having to wait any longer, for here we are. Our feeling of restlessness in life is then an impatience with our not just now having to wait. It is after all the one thing that we were really good at, all those billions of years, our not being anywhere that was once the radical of patience: when a very long time seemed like 'no time at all'.

Not being shows an enormous patience for what might be. It is an almost infinite patience. It *is* an infinite patience.

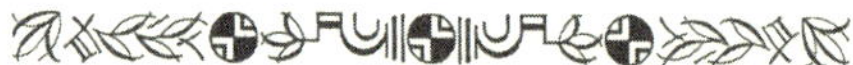

Part of what frightens us is the idea that non-duration itself is something that needs to be endured. Without duration there is no enduring. We find this impossible to imagine, though we were perfectly good at it before we were born. In fact, we were the genius of the fact, its ability to imagine itself, whatever it wasn't.

A painting is always there at the same time as itself.
A story never is.

VII

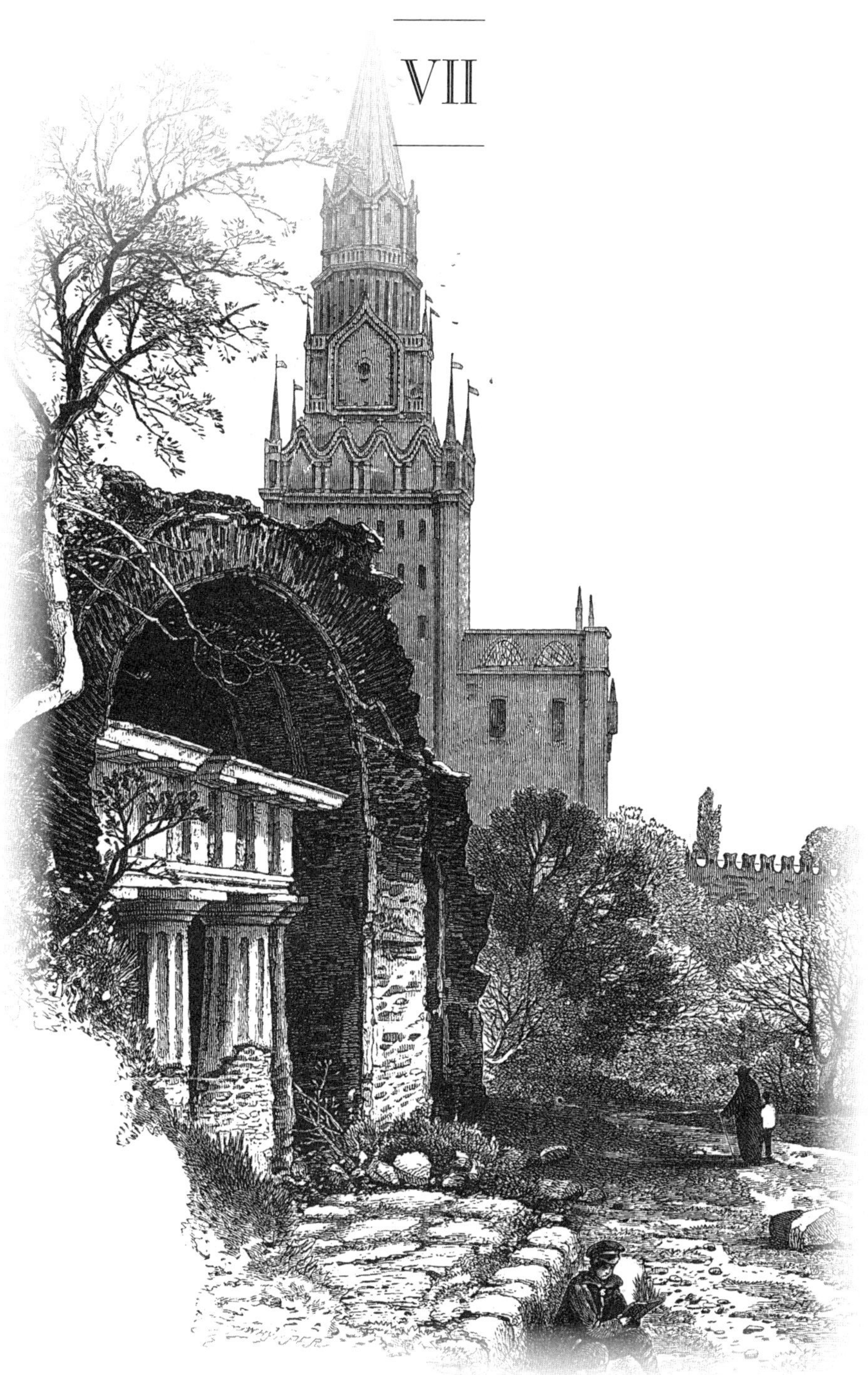

No one living has died yet. The profound naïveté of the whole lot of us wandering about. Most feel that they don't need to die. I mean, they have lived this long and got on just fine without it.

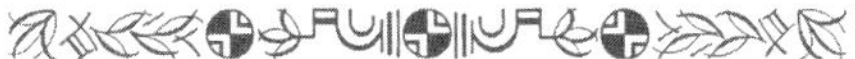

I remember us as children at a swimming pool, hamming it up, divers marching off a diving board with a cheerful salute: our vague sense of pantomime, the broad stride, confident, dismissive of the board's end, and our comic salute as we performed a kind of slapstick pratfall into the water. The courage of one who approaches the end in these terms.

Being dead is our only real way of coping with not being here.

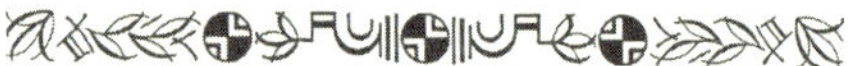

It's a good thing we're dead when we stop breathing. Otherwise we would suffocate.

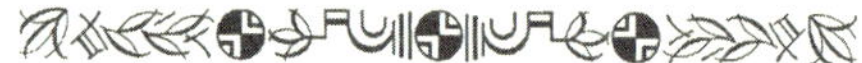

What we need for assisted dying—with cowards like me—is a medication that reproduces one's gradual decline towards death, but in a measured period. You take a pill that will cause you to die in your sleep, say, some time in the next month. It would be much easier to swallow, so to speak. You wouldn't have to feel that you were bludgeoning yourself unconscious at that very instant. I would become an instant insomniac of course.

Philip Larkin's 'Aubade'—on the fear of death—goes about as far as any poem can into the hell that waits for us when we think of our individual consciousness as an end in itself, that that is all there is. After the night sweats, morning comes and Larkin simply recalls our terrifying impotence in the face of certain facts:

> The sky is white as clay, with no sun.
> Work has to be done.
> Postmen like doctors go from house to house.

Of course, that *is* all there is for an individual consciousness, in one sense. But if you can't come around to identify with something larger than the twinkle of your own little star, then 'Aubade' is where you end up.

It wasn't always about the individual. We have lost a little of that subtle deference we once held towards larger social or spiritual orders. The spiritual order itself can easily slip into guarantees for the preservation of our own consciousness ... that thing we fear losing. But in the end God is no respecter of persons. That is the pill that the doctor at the end of the poem, going from house to house, needs to administer.

On having nothing for a subject. It is one of those few fields in which knowing next to nothing about it is not only excusable, but an actual prerequisite.

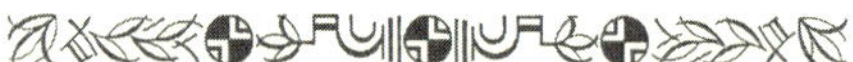

Think of how surprised we would be when we die, if we could feel surprise. To be suddenly not. The mother of all Whoas.

Certain religions say that at the moment of death the mind leaves the body, but in another perspective, the mind becomes the body, becomes the physical conditions that gave rise to it. We fall back into the wholly physical. And the body, which has been running itself to distraction all these years, must stop, go still, and concentrate to receive it.

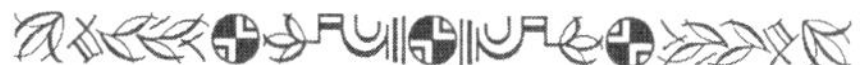

In this sense, consciousness would be the mist and vapours that rise from a boiling soup. They are made of the same substance, the body of the soup and the vapours hovering just over it. The vapours are only the 'highest' expression of its heat. When the heat ends, the mist does not leave the soup, but settles back into it, or better, dissipates by staying where it is.

The proof that you've successfully imagined your death is that you instinctively shudder or turn away from the thought with your whole body. Can one find the verbal formula that gets one to that fleeting glimpse, not as the sensitive tooth you put pressure on to see if the pain is still there, but a revelation of the presence of the thought that cannot be thought?

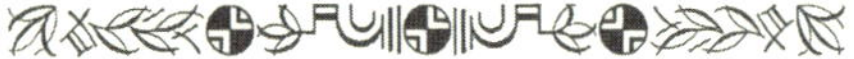

Not wanting to die is the inevitable, natural, and finally very small price of liking it here.

The great characters of fiction live as truly among us as the dead do. It seems then that to enjoy life-after-death one needn't have actually lived.

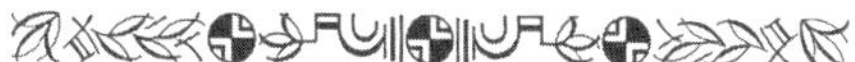

Being at the point of one's own death is like being on the event horizon of a black hole. The nothing is the black hole. We speculate on what, if we could actually experience the moment, it *would be like* to pass over the event horizon: a revelation of all time and space. The fact that we can't experience it doesn't keep it from being *like* something.

This phrase I keep coming back to: oblivion is unstable.

We are gatherings out of the elements. Energies and molecules coalesce for a while into this event called you, and then spend themselves. The principle of the conservation of energy, nothing lost or gained. What comes to be arises out of what already exists. Merely a reshuffling of relations in chemistry and physics. But why are you *you* rather than someone else? Bishop's question in 'In the Waiting Room'. How is it possible to be one and not another? We 'belong to' the particular carbon and hydrogen atoms that make us up. That radical contingency does not bode well for any idea of *transcendent* spirit. It seems to suggest that what we call our own consciousness and being arises out of materials that merely expressed themselves as such and you are that particular *as such*.

But still the mystery. I am not the dandelion over there. I am the minded elements that make up this particular cluster of molecules and when they return to the dust, what happens? There is no waiting for them to recombine into something else. No. Our consciousness 'belongs to' those dispersed chemicals. It would not be you that became conscious again when the chemicals recombined. It would be another chemical batch's 'me', even if it contained exactly the same molecules that make you now. The robin singing cheerup-cheerily outside my window just now is evidently having the same existential crisis.

Something else I have to sort out. Is a stone's nothing-to-itself the same as a plant's nothing-to-itself? Or better, is it the same as your hand's nothing-to-itself? Is the naught of the stone to itself different from the naught of the flower to itself? I'm inclined to say no. So, just as one can be alive and naught, one can be naught and alive. An entry in the book of small consolations.

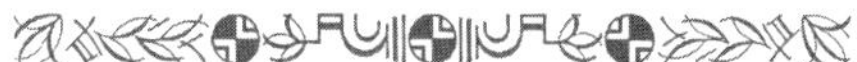

I can't figure out where nowhere is. This seems central. We don't go to a 'where', and yet we leave 'here'. If we leave one place, or if we leave place itself, we end up in a no-place, even if we don't go there. Nowhere is the place we don't go to. We go nowhere in ceasing to be where we are. How far or near? How far or near?

We think we know where the dead are in relation to us, but where are we in relation to the dead? This GO train moving along the Lakeshore. Where is it in relation to my father now? A nothingness has no spatial compass. I am not east or west of him. Where am I? This somewhere in the midst of a nowhere. How would I even set out? And yet these train tracks stretch ahead and behind.

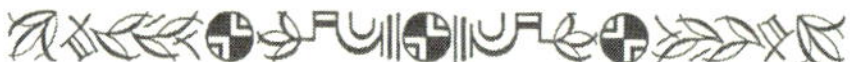

Nothing (that is, not anything) is what it is only in relation to a something that follows or precedes it. Which does not mean that nothing is something. Yet nothing *is* something. It will be 'the thing that is the case'.

Part of the problem is the grammatical construction, 'He is dead.' As though death were a state that was, that had to do with the copula verb and the sort of work it can perform. But of course the grammar is all wrong. It may be a comfort to some that death is not an ontological state of being that can fit in a sentence. Death is *the* grammatical error.

What do you have when you have the absence of absence? Not a presence of course, but not 'absence' either. One may take consolation in the fact that what dies along with presence is absence itself. We will be whatever is 'left over' when these two nouns cancel each other out. Except that to say we will *be* whatever is left over is to get it wrong again. Donne's line, 'Death, thou too shalt die' gets at the more conventional Christian principle, but there is a metaphysics behind it worth daydreaming over. I prefer Shakespeare's formulation: 'And death, once dead, there's no more dying then', with its little grammatical puzzle that leaves us in doubt as to whether it is death that dies ('and death, once it is dead …'), or us ('and death, once we are dead …'). In the end we content ourselves with these little gifts, these little windows, granted by grammatical puzzles.

You hear of suicides in their last hours writing letters, arranging house, settling bills, cleaning up, washing dishes after a full breakfast and so on. The powerful sense that there is a reason to do these things before one disappears. The faith invested in what that might be, even if it is something as simple as 'a world ongoing without me'. This is our version of the Egyptian ritual of providing the dead with 'necessities' for the journey ahead, but in reverse, with things left behind for the living to live on with.

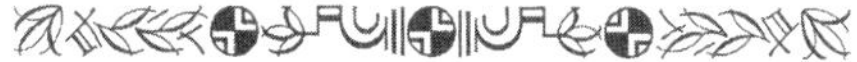

Dying is one of the things you don't have to practise to get right. In any case, you don't get to practise. Your body's accomplishment of its own conclusion will be perfect and complete. Not one part of you will be left living. I've never been that perfect at anything. Unless its opposite also counts, being perfectly alive.

The moment of death as a stained-glass window. Looking at it from the outside—from the perspective of being alive—it appears dark, as nothing. But now just imagine: you are already standing in the midst of what, looking from the inside, the window would colourfully admit, and at a point from which there is no need to look out, for there you aren't.

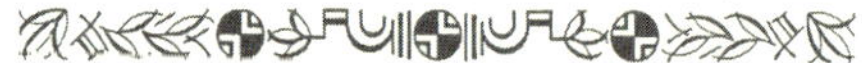

How our nothingness will be a form of patience, a patience with eternity. How quietly we will wait, how peacefully. Is there a patience that can outwait nothingness itself?

That patience partly inheres, in the near term after death, in what remains of us. Shakespeare as a form of patience dwelling inside the journeying of his work among us. But I don't mean for this to intrude on the original sense of patience here, which really dwells at the heart of absence itself. The 'viaticum' of Jankélévitch.

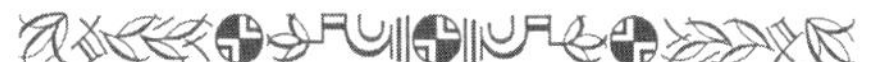

Jankélévitch: 'Once you have been, you can never not have been. From that time on, the mysterious and profoundly obscure fact of having lived will be your viaticum for all eternity.' Viaticum: provisions for a journey. Things you will need. Having-been is a provision for the future as you head off into nothing. There's a recipe there. Subtract from your having-been the possibility of remembering it, then subtract from its future value your ever being conscious of that value. You have the bare bones of the provision. A having-been as something sent forward in the mere fact of its uneraseability, that in spite of all, it will always have been so. The Egyptians buried their dead with little wooden boats to carry them to the next world. Because they were, the boat is. Look at it there, in the tomb or under glass at the museum, sailing on.

Our belatedness, this mere Tuesday afternoon, makes us seem so small and petty. Nothing new under the sun. And yet the dead, when they dreamed of their worldly posterity, their afterlife, dreamed of us, dreamed of this moment that lay in an unimaginable future. Just finished watching Jean Cocteau's wonderful little film, made in 1962, a year before he died, in which he addresses those who will watch his film in the year 2000. How strange and otherworldly that world seemed to him. Do you still have tables, do you still use language, can you watch this film? But he felt it was important to look towards it. There's a typology there. We fulfill, just by being here, what in Cocteau's present moment was latent or apparently missing, a revelation of his 'ends'. But we depend on him in order to feel 'arrived at'. Whitman was getting at the same thing at the end of 'Song of Myself'. He addresses us in the future, but says, 'I stop somewhere, waiting for you.'

This strange sense in which we are resurrected into the minds of those who read us. When we lived, we gave a language to a series of conscious synapses, an algorithm or a narrative. That series is set to work once more as it unfolds in the brain of the later one who reads it. But so what? I put myself into words, as we say. The words are taken up into a living mind after I am gone. My original consciousness is extracted from the old words and made to course through a later living mind. A programmer generates code, a software. The software lies dormant, and then is taken up again and 'realized' in a later computer. The point is presumably then that we have to identify ourselves with the software, the product of the programmer's programming. But we don't. We identify with the programmer's *activity* of generating code. How close, how very close, the software comes to being an instantiation of the original process that made it. Does the original really need to last in its own right? It has found something better. It has perpetuated what it makes and what can be made of what it makes.

The value of prolonging the original process is minimal indeed. It is superfluous in every deep sense. We identify so much with the maker over the made. Contemporary sceptical criticisms are egotistical in just this way. You demonize the products of culture and invest instead in your own living, ironizing work as it finds flaws in what came before. Always a 'that is not me' in our examination of cultural products. Look at what this one who came before me has done wrong. And what is more, watch me demonize my own cultural products. I too am nothing! Think of how powerful I must be to erase myself even as I say what I say! I must be some sort of god.

But we all die into what we have made. We live only in the record of our having been. Our very processes of mind are recorded there. Our very thoughts. An order of synapses that unfolded may unfold again. And maybe, because we ourselves will then be in the midst of an absolute naught, we are, in a sense yet to be understood, resurrected in the minds of others for the very reason that we will be *nothing else* at that time. At present we feel ourselves to be so 'something else besides' that we cannot see, nor intuit, nor understand, much less experience, how this 'resurrected life' is as genuine a form of life as any. The poem, the software, the DNA … they not only re-exist, as it were, but continue to summon their own potential for always more. What you make here and now, when it is later rediscovered, is the instantiation, there and then, of that more-life coming clear. Makes one think of Moses again and his view of the promised land that he himself would never enter.

Living on in others, or at least in what lives on, is only unsatisfying if you think you are *in* you. The question is not *who*, but *where* do you think you are?

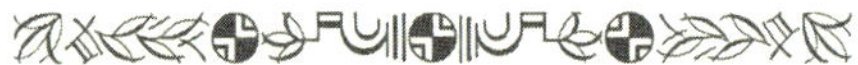

The extent to which we live by reputation is the extent to which we intuit a 'realer' self abiding among others. The ancients understood this. A self that has agency, effect, a history, a still-active creative power, and a future that follows after every least thing we do. That realer self is a collection of the things done that you drop as you go, like the pebbles of Hansel and Gretel: their future stretching out behind them.

Was thinking of this line, 'We leave you behind.' Of course, it isn't true. There is a no-time just 'on the other side' of time. When we die we pass into it, but do not recede. It is not part of a time that *can* recede. It is there 'with' us. There is a door that gives onto it at every instant. All the dead, from all time, are just on the other side of that door. They are nothing there, but they do not go away.

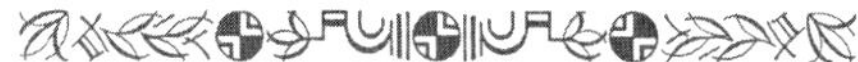

Once dead, your not-being is as near to the time of Shakespeare, even to Shakespeare himself, as it is to someone who died the same day as you. Your not-being is as close to the farthest galaxy as it is to your bedpost.

Proust was here about a second ago. The moment of death 'passes' in such a way for the deceased that all time afterwards is but the next instant. We are inside that next instant, at his bedside.

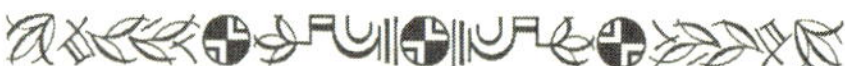

This idea of authors living on in their writing. Think of how we speak of earlier works as though the authors were doing what they were doing here and now. So, two hundred years from now, a writer might still say, 'Here we see how Elizabeth Bishop introduces the problem of....' What Bishop has done continues to be done, long after Bishop has stopped doing it.

Look at the words we have written and that appear now in print. Think about how those marks on the page, as marks on a page, are *so not breathing*. Think of how, if we were like those words on the page, we would suffocate and die. The terrible non-living state in which our living thoughts abide. Lowell's 'my open book, my open coffin'. Now think of how, when we die and stop breathing, we become like the words on the page. And yet I just finished saying that something lives in them.

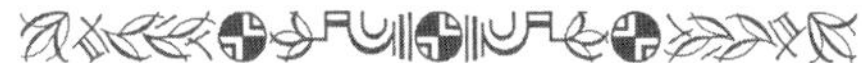

They leave their work behind in the no-space and the no-where of their after-death. Their work joins all works, in the same place as the *Iliad*, *King Lear*, 'The Wood-Pile'. In the same way, they themselves join Homer, Shakespeare, Frost, all in the same 'time'. The work and the person, from this non-perspective, occupy the same non-place. Can non-places be similar? Are all non-places one?

Just reading Ben Franklin's Last Will and Testament and thinking about how the will itself bespeaks a certain implied understanding of one's 'afterlife' in society and among one's relations. We extend that part of our being that is perhaps most precious to us and potentially lasting: that is, our agency. After we die what we made of ourselves continues to have purchase in the world of human culture. The will in a sense arranges for this agency within its small sphere. Preferable to just thinking of it as cleaning up after ourselves, or a fire sale.

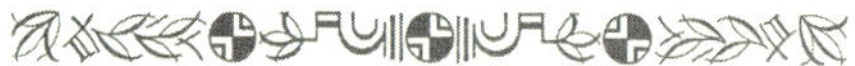

The fact of your book now in the hands of an unknown reader and the fact of the book being read after you've died. It is the same fact. In Red Deer a woman is sitting in a chair with your book. It is and must always be nothing to you, since you know nothing of it. In that sense your afterlife has already started, over there in Red Deer.

Our fear of death is a measure of our inability to imagine and identify with the hereness of others.

You follow your parents into the world and they nurse you into adulthood, show you how to be in the world by already being in it themselves, a fact that you find enormously impressive and reassuring. Then you age and the process goes into reverse. They become less and less able to function in the world and you nurse them back into an innocence. Then it goes into reverse again on the other side of experience. They die and in dying show you how.

Afterwards you find it hard to be afraid of something that someone you love dearly has actually gone through themselves. Here, they say. Like this.

You will never know that you are not. The only thing you will *ever* know is that you are. A kind of makeshift immortality, the infinite within a confined space. Stevens' 'A glass aswarm with things going as far as they can.'

VIII

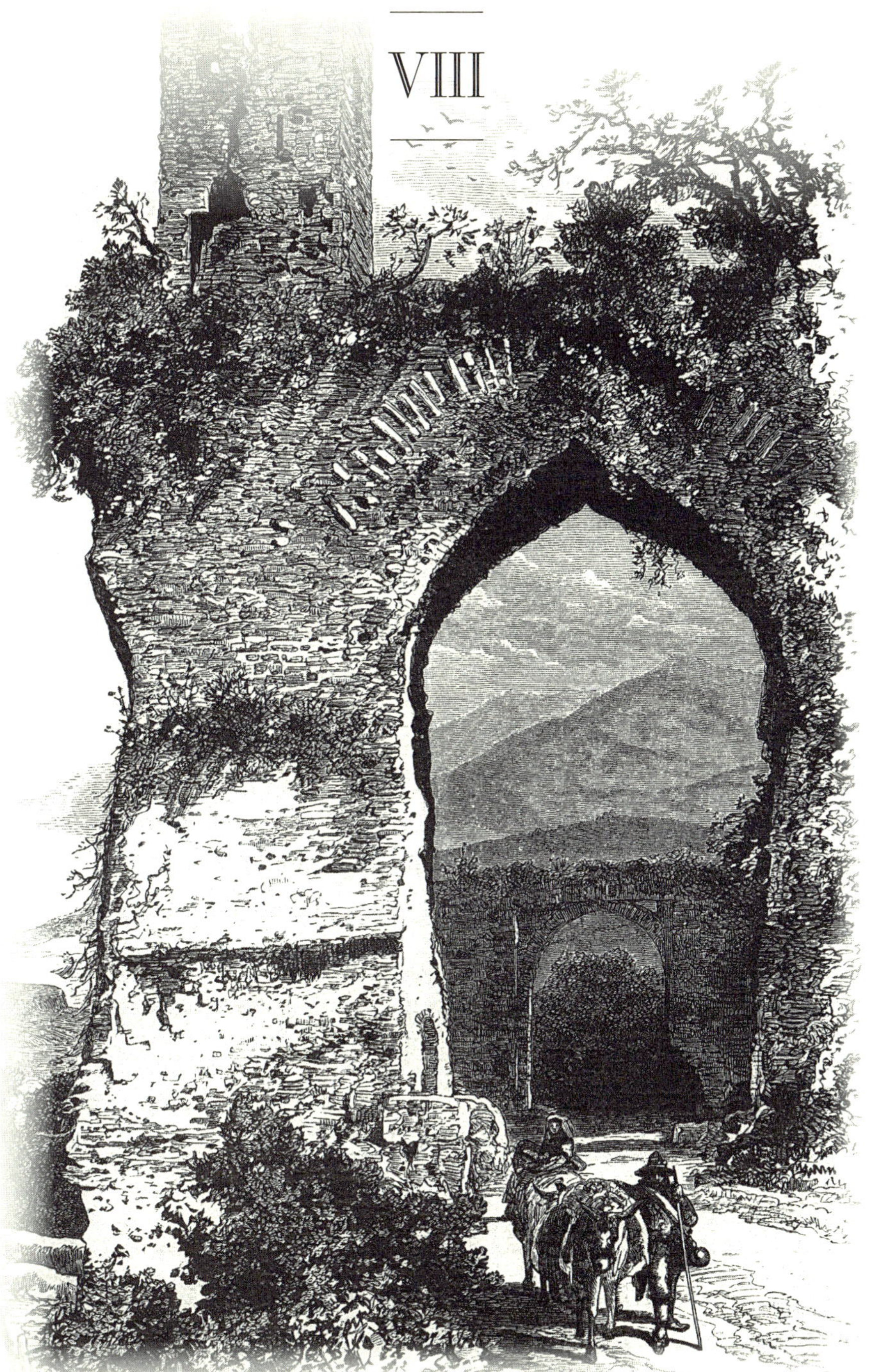

All this trouble Aspies have with planning and organization, specifically with taking smaller steps towards a larger goal. My trouble writing extended monographs, the block I hit when I start thinking about writing the least paragraph towards an unseen result. But surely the scribble-and-go approach could be part of the way around this. Notebooks are filled with arguments that are not ready to be arguments, but are ready at least to be themselves.

I wonder what the stupidest thing is that I've ever done. Everyone would have one, no matter how careful they were. Among the many stupid things that I might recall, one would be the stupidest, one would win, one would pull ahead of the other almost-as-stupid things, and shine. Some would know with certainty what their stupidest thing was. Others like me would have many stupid things crowding at the end for a photo finish. Imagine being the stupid thing that places, say, fourth.

We spend most of our days giving other people proof of our flaws. We have no idea how generous we are.

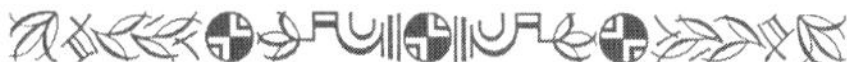

You can do great evil using a part of your imagination, but it is harder to do great evil using all of it.

The moment you feel that you are right beyond any doubt, your imagination has failed you.

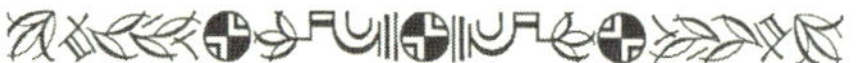

How innocent one's children are. They sit in the back of the car, strapped in. You drive along and turn left. They drive along and turn left. You turn in at the grocery store. They turn in at the grocery store. I find it heartbreaking.

What people experience is not so much your love for them, as your capacity for love generally. The two are often confused.

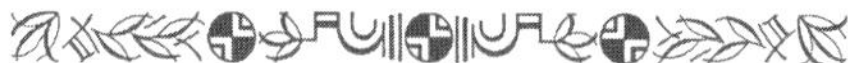

How the river dreamed, after hearing Heraclitus, that it was a foot.

A man stands at the edge of a flat empty field. He says, 'There must be a way across, but I do not know how to find it.'

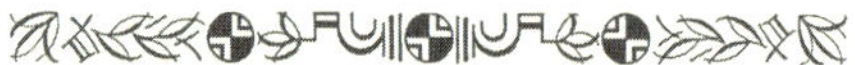

First buds of spring. The sense that nature does not have a memory, though it seems as though it does. It recalls what leaves are like.

When does the end not come suddenly? But I think of the courage of snow. It falls gently for hours then says, 'Enough', and goes, just in time for the air to clear.

About the Author

Jeffery Donaldson is the author of six collections of poetry, most recently *Fluke Print* (Porcupine's Quill, 2018). His book *Palilalia* (McGill-Queen's, 2008) was a finalist for the Canadian Authors Association Award for Poetry. Donaldson has also written works of criticism on poetry and metaphor. He lives on the Niagara Escarpment near Grimsby. He teaches poetry and American literature at McMaster University.